As The

Butterbeans Boil

Recollections and Recipes

By

Jayme Washington

Smalley

ii

Cover Design by

Tobia Hawklyn

Printed in the United States of America

Library of Congress   TXU 844-018

February, 2, 1998

ISBN 1 – 4116 – 1081 – 4

For Emma, Hattie, Warren
and
Brooks

Acknowledgements

I would like to express appreciation to my mother, Emma Douse Washington, and my grandparents, Hattie Washington Douse and Willie Warren Douse. This book was possible thanks to their excellent ability to describe their life experiences in interesting and memorable ways.

I would like to thank all the family, friends and teachers in my childhood who allowed me to pester them with endless questions. (I'd also like to express my appreciation to the makers of Coca-Cola and Goody Headache Powders).

Special thanks to Deborah Moody and her mother Myrtle Woods, now deceased, who convinced me these stories needed to be shared and kept me on task.

Sylvia, Ellen, Thelma, Cherie, Katherine, Wayne, Joanne, Gary, Jennie, Peggy, Ellis, Ann, Marriane, Queen Esther, Cheryl, Gil, Jane, John, Nancy, Pat, Dianne, Mary, Claudette, Kim, Don, Betty, Barbara, Marj, P.D., Tobia, Mike, Edward and Mark will all know why their names are listed here.

I am very appreciative to Brooks for having to do things his own way and giving me cause to design more innovative ways to explain situations that weren't based on incredible amounts of logic.

As The Butterbeans Boil

Introduction

Jamersinz Emily Washington thinks she's the richest kid on the planet! Jayme (as she prefers to be called) is convinced she has plenty of all the important things in life: family, friends and good food.

She wants to know everything you know in one hour or less. Wherever Jayme chooses to be, there are adults well acquainted with headaches, and kids who know a lot more than they did before she arrived.

She loves to read, cook, sew, knit, crochet, do needlework, draw pictures, play the piano, sing, write and compose what she calls *Witty Ditties*. (Grown folks call them poems). She has no time for games except jack-stones and an occasional rickrack. Jayme is certain that everyone in the world is equally talented and her abilities are nothing special. Her loving family, gifted in their own right, wants to make sure she fits in, so they allow her fantasy to continue.

Young Jayme manages to pick joy and laughter from the weeds of segregation rooted in the South during the late 1950's.

As The Butterbeans Boil is a fond look back as well as a continuing saga of discovery................

-Jayme Washington Smalley

Table of Contents

<u>*Recipes*</u>

All Aboard!

Your suitcase is packed. Your trunk's been gone.
You're lying in bed, now what you waiting on?
There's cooking, sewing and other chores to tend.
You can't just lie there like you're on the mend.

Get out of that bed girl; the day is passing you by.
There're thousands of new things for you to try.

Books on the shelves are calling out to be read.
I cannot believe you're still lying in bed!

Roll over and rub the sleep from your eyes.
Missing the train at this station
Won't get you the prize.

Your suitcase is packed. Your trunk's been gone.
You're lying in bed, now what you waiting on?

The Birthday Book

Sometimes I really don't like being a kid! Somebody's always yelling for you to move from wherever you are, or stop doing something you like to do. Grown folks refuse to listen to anything you say, unless you happen to be hollering that something's on fire. (Even then you'd probably get blamed for starting it).

I like to know why people do and say the things they do, so I ask lots of questions. I don't see anything wrong with that, but Momma tells me I can be a pest and give people headaches. She says I want to know too much too fast and I don't give grown folks time to think about the right thing to say to a kid. I'm supposed to be quiet, listen more and talk less. Sometimes when we go out, Momma looks down over her glasses and cuts the whites of her eyes in my direction. (She calls it, *giving me the white eye*). If I keep talking, she pinches me when nobody's looking. I know better than to holler because I'd really get into big trouble.

I had to figure out something else to do besides talk and ask questions. I decided eating would cause a lot less trouble. I love to talk, but I'd rather eat! I like the feeling of good food going down my gullet (that's what Granddad calls my throat), and the food around here is always good. No matter what's going on in our house, no one argues during meals. All is right with the world at our big oak dinner table.

In the center of the table is a tall beige, fluted glass dish. Grandma Hattie says its Carnival Glass. She and her sister-in-law, Miss Lizzie each bought one for twenty-five cents at the opening of Woolworth's on Broad Street in downtown Augusta. I used to think the bowl was made onto the table, but now I know they just keep putting it back in the same place.

I live in Augusta, Georgia with my Momma, Granddad and Grandma. My father was killed in an auto accident and Momma decided I'd be better off in the South than in downtown Philadelphia where we were living. My Grandparents and Momma were living in Sunset Homes Apartments and they'd loved it at first. All the up and coming colored people lived there, including the president of Paine College. There were tennis courts, playgrounds and even a tenant council. My Momma ran the nursery school and loved every minute of it. She left to be with my father in Philadelphia because he told her things were better up there. Momma hated to leave Sunset because she and my grandparents had wonderful friends like the Lamars. I think Miss Thelma looks like a movie star! She plays the piano and Momma and her are still buddies.

Sometime after the end of World War II, the government took over Sunset and anyone who needed housing could move in. Grandma and Granddad were more than ready to move out. When I was three, Momma sent money for a down payment on a house we could all share.

Grandma Hattie picked out this double tenement on Wooten Road. There's a hall down the middle and each twosome has it's own side. The house was built quickly for a lady in the community about to have a baby at any minute. The neighbors didn't know much about being carpenters; so using rulers and levels was out. Momma wasn't happy when she saw the house for the first time, but the deal was done and it was important for us to be together.

My Granddaddy, Warren Douse, does cleaning and yard work for people. His main job is preaching and he knows more about the Bible than any person alive! He goes around Georgia and South Carolina preaching at churches so far in the backwoods, Momma says you need a search warrant to find them! Grandma Hattie works for Miss Josie, who lives on the hill, where most of the rich white folks are. They've known each other since they were girls. Grandma does a little dusting and fixes lunch, but mostly she keeps Miss Josie company. Momma works for the City Recreation Department at Gilbert Manor Housing Project. She gets to do lots of different things like have Playschool in the mornings and teach crafts and sewing in the afternoons. There isn't anything my Momma can't do.

There's always something going on at our house. Granddaddy's church members like to stop in and visit and there aren't many people on Wooten Road who haven't tasted Grandma's cooking. We have more than enough food. We raise chickens, turkeys and ducks and have fruit trees of all kinds: pear, plum, apple and a huge grape arbor. Grandma grows any vegetable she can find a seed for. Our neighbors, the Jacksons, raise pigs and have a smokehouse to cure the meat. They give us pork and we give them poultry and eggs.

Granddad's church members love to share whatever they have with us too. If we aren't home, they leave boxes and bags of different things on the pump house out back. I'm not allowed to sniff, complain or ask what's in any of the stuff we get. One time we came home to find a box with corn, fig preserves and some gray-looking meat wrapped in foil. It was tasty, but a bit on the stringy side. Later we found out it was barbecued goat. We'd never had goat before, but we always say *Thank you* and keep on chewing.

Grandma's brother Tom loves to hunt and fish and he shares what he gets with us. He's left possum, rabbit, deer, catfish, and eels on the pump house. My great uncle says the eels grab the bait off the hook and are a real pain, but every now and then, he nets one for his precious *Sus* to fry. (Every one of Grandma's eight living brothers and sisters call her that). She says with so much food around it would be a sin to even think about complaining.

On July 17th Grandma Hattie gave me this
pretty pink book. She told me I should write down
stories I've heard, recipes and anything else I might
think of. I love to make words rhyme. (Grandma
calls them poems, but they drive Momma crazy)! I
call them *Witty Ditties.* I'm not sure what good it's
going to do, but Grandma's hopeful writing will
keep me out of trouble. My handwriting is good
and I read any and everything I can get my hands
on. Besides that, I ask a whole lot of questions.
The first time I wrote in this book it seemed a little
silly, but the more I write, the more I like it. It's
great that I can write with one hand and eat with the
other.

Everybody in my house is a good cook.
(I've heard there're people who can't cook at all,
but I've never met anyone in such a fix and I don't
believe they're real). Momma tells me, when I was
little, she stood me on a soapbox in our kitchen in
Philly, so I could see what she was doing. I have
my own cake pans, cookie molds and pots. I know
how to follow a recipe, but most times everyone
around here cooks and measures from memory.
Momma just knows how much salt is in a teaspoon

full. I have to ask Grandma to slow down cooking so I can write down what she puts in the pot or the bowl.

People in the projects are always talking about their stories like *As The World Turns.* I have my own soap opera going on, and I get to write it all down. I think *As The Butterbeans Boil* is just as interesting as anything on TV. Each of my family members thinks of themselves as a good storyteller and has their favorite tales and characters.

Grandma Hattie is the oldest girl of a family of thirteen. She makes everyone laugh with stories from her childhood home, near a swamp in South Carolina that's now the Savannah River Site. (We call it the bomb plant). Granddaddy could fill the Wallace Branch Library with all the tales he tells. Just keeping up with some of the churches he goes to and the people he meets would be a full time job.

Momma loves to tell me about when she was growing up. She and her two best pals ate anything that didn't eat them first! All three kids were called by their first and middle names. *The Little Rascals* were tame compared to Emma Addie, John Lewis and James Howard, the *Washpot Gang.*

I've heard all about how difficult it was for everyone during the Depression. Augusta, Georgia is on the Savannah River and there have been many floods. The one in 1929 was especially bad and Momma's family ended up living at the courthouse until the water went down. I'm always hearing about my Daddy and how he was in World War II. I love the stories about me! I managed to cause confusion coming into the world and according to Granddad; I'm still at it.

When I hear the stories, I feel like I was there when it was all happening. Since we have so much fun cooking and eating, I'm making sure I write down the recipes for all my favorites. I will definitely run out of pages in this book before I run out of stories and good eats to share.

Hard Knocks Glue

Hattie Washington and Warren Douse shared the same secret as they grew up. They both wanted to be somewhere else. Grandma Hattie was the oldest girl at home and her folks, Papa Guvnor and Donnie expected her to carry on the business of the household. Granddad Warren had his hands full taking care of his three brothers and one sister. His mother died when he was nine and his father, Sailor Douse, married a much younger woman, who everyone called Cousin Pig. She was interested in Mr. Douse's money and didn't like his children. I know my Grandparents love each other, but I've never seen them hold hands or kiss. Granddad says they're glued together by hard knocks.

Grandma's oldest brother Obie, moved to Augusta, married Laura and had baby Annie. It wasn't long before Hattie married Warren and made the same move with baby Emma. Grandma adores her brother and loves to tell me how they helped each other when they were growing up. In the fields, Obie would put extra cotton in his sister's sack so she'd make her one hundred pounds for the day. When it was time to weed, Hattie would hoe her brother's rows because she was faster at that job.

The fun in Augusta stopped suddenly when Laura died a few months after giving birth to her second child, Rebecca. Obie didn't think he would ever recover from losing his wife, but the family pulled together as usual and made it through the tough times. Her Grandmother Donnie took in baby Rebecca and Annie moved in with her Aunt Hattie, Uncle Warren and Cousin Emma. No matter what was going on, somebody would think of something to laugh about. My Grandma loves telling this story and I never get tired of hearing it.

The Chimney Sweep

Papa Guvnor and Donnie liked to spend time at the docks of the Savannah River. One morning early they left for their favorite place and lost track of the time. The children were at the house with no food cooked. George was the oldest boy at home, but Tom, the next oldest, was smart as a whip. Grandma Donnie loved her chickens and the children knew they weren't supposed to bother them. As the day wore on, the stomach growling got louder and Tom got bolder.

Before anyone realized what was happening, Tom grabbed a fat speckled hen from the yard and chopped the head off! He began giving orders to the others to get wood for the stove, and bowls for mixing. Hunger calmed their fear and moved their feet because in no time, the hen was in a pot and the kitchen smelled like chicken and dumplings.

When the cooking was done, the kids ate like pigs at a trough. When the last dumpling was sopped up, they began to wonder what kind of story they could tell their Momma about why her prize hen was missing. All of a sudden, Tom got a strange look on his face and ran outside. He took the ladder from the other side of the barn and set it up against the house. He asked the children to help him catch another chicken and they chased down a light colored one, about the same size as the one they'd eaten.

Tom got a long piece of rope from the barn. He used it to tie the chicken's feet together and then loop it around the body. He called for the children to steady the ladder. As he climbed up slowly, clutching the chicken under his arm, they had no idea what he was up to.

Tom carefully made his way to the roof. He crept towards the chimney, leaned over and began to lower the chicken down. It disappeared and the children could only see their brother, moving the rope from side to side and dipping it up and down. The hen's loud squawking sounded funny coming from inside the chimney. Finally the squawking became louder as Tom pulled the chicken up over the top brick.

There was a shout of joy! The hen was speckled with chimney soot and looked just like the one they'd eaten! Everyone on the ground clapped, cheered and danced around! Tom hurried down the ladder and cut the soot-covered chicken loose. Everyone helped clean up the kitchen and finished just as they heard the jingling of the bells on their folks' wagon. Papa Guvnor and Donnie were very tired and went right to bed.

The next day, all eyes were on Donnie when she went out to feed the chickens. Everyone held their breath as she made the usual clucking noises and scattered the feed around the yard. They were very relieved when she didn't notice anything different.

The hen was fine until rain washed off some of the soot. The feathers turned a horrible grayish color but it had been too long, and the adults didn't remember what the other chicken looked like.

(The children whispered this story among themselves until they were grown and it was much too late for anybody to get a whipping!)

Calling for Emma

Grandma Hattie still complains about missing the Thanksgiving Day Barbeque. She had her mouth all tuned up for pulled pork and hash and rice, but the baby she was having had other ideas. Emma Addie Douse had to get into the world on November 28, 1918 and she didn't mind that her mother's plans had to be changed. According to Momma, there're many chickens, mules and cows that answer when someone calls out the name Emma. For as long as I can remember, my Momma has complained about having such a common name.

From Jackson, South Carolina, the family crossed the Savannah River to Augusta, Georgia, and settled in the downtown section. They made friends quickly and everyone shared good times and bad.

Since Granddad Warren could read and write, he got a job in the office at Merry Brothers Brick Company, doing errands and carrying papers where they needed to go. He wore hand me down suits from Mr. Merry himself. When the Depression hit, the white man who had been his boss got his job.

Granddad found himself hacking bricks on the line outside. The hard work and humiliation were too much and he left the brickyard to take up preaching, cleaning and selling bananas. Miss hattie took in washing and ironing because, tough times or not, there were just some jobs white people wouldn't do for themselves.

Even the slow moving Savannah River, rose up to make things more difficult. The floodwaters didn't pick who drowned by their color. To save itself, the whole town had to work together. Hard times mad families' stories easier to remember.

The Washpot Gang

Emma Addie, James Howard and John Lewis played all over downtown Augusta and were well known in their neighborhood near Cedar Grove Cemetery. Together the three were brave against any danger and not even ghost stories from their friend Mr. Dave kept the children from scampering too long among the headstones in the colored section. James Howard's Grandma, Miss Wooden swore the three had cast iron stomachs, like washpots. She said they would "e*at anything that didn't eat them first"* and started calling them the Washpot Gang.

There wasn't a fruit tree around that hadn't been stripped bare by the Gang at some time. Emma Addie, the leader, would go to the owner and ask if they could pick the fruit on halves. The owner would get half of whatever was picked and the Gang would split the other half three ways. The only problem was the kids could eat ten times their weight in fruit while they picked! They'd hide extra sacks in the bushes and tote them off at the end of the picking.

Sometimes the Gang played with Junior, a crippled white boy, who lived downtown with his grandmother. They liked Junior well enough, but he had a mean streak about him, especially if he didn't get his way. His mother died hours after he was born, and there was gossip his daddy was in the Klan. Taking care of Junior fell to his grandmother.

Junior's Nanaw, as he called her, turned the Gang loose to pick up pecans in her yard. Junior hopped around the huge yard on his crutches, going after pecans like he was at an Easter egg hunt. By lunchtime he had a respectable pile of nuts. James Howard and John Lewis were careful to hide the extra sacks in the hedges while Junior was trying to get the pecans to go where he wanted them. He'd pick out a pecan, hold up on one leg, and try to hit it with the tip end of one of his crutches. Sometimes he landed on the ground, but when his Nanaw wasn't around to make a fuss, he picked himself up and started over.

The Gang taught Junior how to shoot marbles. Even though Nanaw fussed about his scraped knuckles, it didn't stop him from getting a nice collection of cat's eyes. Nanaw was more than happy for the Gang to entertain Junior because it meant a little time of peace when he wasn't fussing and cussing at her. She didn't mind serving them tomato sandwiches and lemonade. The tomatoes came from her small garden in the back but there was nothing small about them. Junior and the Gang would eat the juicy sandwiches under the shade of the pecan tree. They would have almost as much tomato on their clothes as in their stomachs!

Junior refused to let Nanaw be around when he was playing with the Gang. If she lingered too long, he'd holler, *Git away Nanaw*! *Ain't you got women's business to tend to in the house?* If he caught her peeping out the kitchen curtains, he'd throw a rock near the window.

By late afternoon the pecan tree and the yard were nearly clear. That day the Gang helped Junior pick up his pile of pecans, but he insisted they play marbles before they left. Emma Addie drew the ring with a stick and the game went on without a hitch until James Howard won one of Junior's favorite marbles. He went into a fit and spat, cussed and hopped around. The Gang usually let him have his way, but James Howard wasn't giving in.

Junior flew into a bigger rage and told the Gang he'd tell Nanaw about their sacks hidden in the bushes. The Gang gathered their pickings in a hurry and ran out of the yard with Junior limping after them, screaming ugly names. Nanaw came out the kitchen door when she heard all the noise. Junior was happy to hop over to the bushes and show her one of the sacks of pecans the Gang had hidden. Emma Addie, James Howard and John Lewis were hiding on the other side of the hedges and heard Junior whine, *See Nanaw, the niggers didn't get 'em all!*

The Gang didn't come around to play with Junior for quite a spell. When they did come back, he was so glad to see them, he didn't mind the beating they gave him for calling them names and giving up one of their hiding places.

James Howard's Grandma, Miss Wooden told the Gang the Depression meant there was less money to be had and it didn't buy as much as it used to. She said some white folks were having a hard time being poor and going without. That wasn't news for Negroes and according to Miss Wooden they could get through the hard times if they helped each other. All the families in the neighborhood shared everything they had.

On certain days of the week, Miss Wooden would head up Fifth Street to the A&P Grocery Store, where they'd give her a basket of fruits and vegetables that hadn't sold the day before. She didn't refuse anything and took the Gang along to tote the food home. Absolutely nothing went to waste and anything that couldn't be eaten right away got canned for another time.

The Wash Pot Gang was good at collecting free food. All they had to do was show up with a bucket and the dairy on Greene Street filled it with buttermilk. The local potato chip factory gave hot, greasy brown sacks of broken chips that couldn't be used in the regular bags. They looked terrible, but tasted good and that's all the Gang cared about.

Feeding hungry working people was no easy job, and the Gang was called on to shell peas and beans, shuck corn, crack nuts and peel fruits and vegetables. Sometimes the work was fun, like when they dug bait and sat on the riverbank waiting for the catfish to take a nibble.

James Howard's father, Mr. Brinson, drove a truck for a fruit company. Each evening the Gang collected bananas that fell from bunches. The next day they decided to see just how many ways they could eat them. They made banana pancakes for breakfast, and peanut butter, mayonnaise and banana sandwiches for lunch. For supper they ate fried bananas, banana bread and banana puddin' for dessert. It was weeks before the Gang got up the nerve to even look at another banana!

The Gang got a visit from Etha Bea, James Howard's cousin. She was a sickly little child, and before letting them loose in the neighborhood, Miss Wooden told their visitor how she'd stayed awake at night making teas and other home remedies, to coax out fruit pits, fish bones and even coins from one end or the other of the Gang. She warned Etha Bea that her stomach was no match for guts made of cast iron.

When Emma Addie, James Howard and John Lewis climbed into the fruit truck that afternoon, Etha Bea got in too. The eating went on for quite some time and the Gang, as full as ticks on a dog, hopped out to look for another adventure.

Etha Bea seemed to be asleep, so they left her in the truck.

It was hard dark by the time anyone realized Etha Bea wasn't with the Gang or in the house. The kids remembered where they'd left her and everyone ran in that direction. The poor child couldn't move an inch! She was so clogged up with bananas, the doctor had to be called. They worked through the night and between the doctor's medicine and Miss Wooden's prayers and potions, Etha Bea lived to tell about what happened.

Emma Addie, James Howard and John Lewis slept through the whole thing. Mr. Brinson wanted to wake them up for a whipping, but Miss Wooden came to their rescue. She said Etha Bea was just trying to fit in. The Gang got off with a warning and decided Etha Bea could tag along only if she promised not to eat anything.

Cat's Eyes for Zion

Emma Addie was the first person in her house to hear the bells. She rubbed her eyes and reached for a jumper as she headed toward the front door. All the noise was coming from the direction of the church. The entire neighborhood was starting to move quickly past her house and James Howard and John Lewis waved as they darted in an out of the crowd.

Young Zion Baptist Church was on fire. The flames had destroyed most of the building by the time people realized what was happening. Folks in their nightclothes cried, prayed and hugged each other as they watched. The fire department tried to calm the flames, but it was too late for any part of the building to be saved.

As soon as the smoke cleared, the Washpot Gang was determined to find out how the fire got started. While poking around in the ashes, they found a gasoline can behind a pile of tin and bricks. When the fire chief drove up, they gave him the can so he could catch the person that had burnt Zion down.

Days turned into weeks and no one heard anything about the gasoline can. The fire was ruled an accident and the Board of Deacons collected on the insurance claim. All the money went into the empty treasury and work was quickly begun on a new building.

The Gang took to playing marbles every day in front of the church because they were determined to make sure no more fires broke out. Everything was going along nicely, but there was a spot over the doorway that needed some kind of decoration.

One of the workmen had an idea. He asked the Gang if they wanted to do something for the church. They couldn't wait to help in any way they could. The man asked each of them for some marbles, and the Gang gave up their most colorful cats' eyes and shooters.

The workman built a wooden box around a garbage can lid. He filled it with cement and began arranging the marbles in a sunburst pattern. A large red and white shooter was picked for the center.

When the new creation was dry, the whole neighborhood watched the men lift it into the space over the doorway. No one had ever seen anything quite so beautiful! The sunlight danced through the marbles and it seemed God Himself was lighting the way for folks to come into the new Greater Young Zion Missionary Baptist Church. For weeks the Gang played around Forsythe Street. They loved looking at their gift to Zion and were determined to make sure it stayed safe.

The Ballad of Limber Lee

Mr. Dave tells great stories, the Washpot Gang
agrees.
They sit hours and hours as Dave shoots the breeze.
He tells them of haints, goblins and ghosts.
Sometimes he talks of the Heavenly Hosts.

It doesn't matter to the Gang, they take it all in.
According to them, Dave is free from sin.
Like a momma bird with tiny chicks,
He gives them food and their hunger is fixed.

Their mouths and their minds open wide.
Mr. Dave puts all kinds of thoughts inside.
He tells them of lynching
And public hangings gone wrong.
Dave even sings an occasional song!

His favorite story was a sad one indeed.
How he got into trouble satisfying his greed.
The Gang almost knows the tale by heart.
It only takes a few drinks for Dave to start.

Limber Lee was a bad apple, rotten to the core.
He stole, drank, gambled, cheated and swore.
He had a white girlfriend he met late at night.
No one could give Limber Lee a fright.

That offense alone was enough to condone,
A price upon the villain's head.
Not many would take up a challenge so great.
Mr. Dave was determined to step up to the plate.

He wanted the money and the fame he'd claim,
For bringing the bully down.
It was Saturday night and Dave knew his mark,
Would surely be out on the town.

Many a man and a few women too,
Carried scars from Limber Lee's blade.
Mr. Dave decided when he started out,
No such mistake would be made.

He found Limber Lee in the first place he looked;
A juke joint off the main path.
Dave's pistol was loaded, and so was he
With booze- ready for Limber Lee's wrath.

The men went out to the back of the place,
To shoot dice up against a wall.
The game heated up, steamy as the night.
Limber Lee made the next call.

He spotted a six but he rolled an eight,
Then declared the game was over.
Dave called him a cheat and many quick feet
Moved bodies from drunk to sober.

Limber Lee pulled his knife, but a bullet took his
life.
The police came and took Dave away.
He was walking around bold before his victim got
cold,
But he's sorry to this day.

Oh children mind your Momma! Stay away from
vice.
Don't take what you cannot return.
Limber Lee's spirit saps life from Dave.
His only relief will be the grave.
The two will argue together in hell.
This story is ended there's no more to tell.

All Jacked Up

Obie Washington's second marriage was to a quiet lady everyone called Miss Lizzie. She put the family back together by collecting Annie from her Aunt Hattie and Rebecca from her Grandma Donnie. Miss Lizzie then added Leroy, Ellen and Obie, Jr. to the crowd.

Everyone in the Washington family worked in the wood yard. Obie Washington, Sr. hadn't cared for hacking bricks at Merry Brothers, so he started his own business. There was plenty to be done because most people in the community kept warm by burning wood in the small heaters called trash burners. The heaters usually sat in the middle of the room on pieces of tin or brick platforms. People had to have wood for cooking meals and heating water. Wood was almost as valuable as gold.

Jack was a big, rather shaggy-looking mutt with a friendly personality. He was expected to do his part by guarding the business. Customers were used to seeing him wagging his tail as he came forward to get his head patted.

Leroy and Obie Jr. were Jack's best buddies and he walked them to school every day. Jack would make sure they were inside safely before he'd return to the wood yard. Sometimes he'd ride in the truck during deliveries. He was known for sometimes jumping down to chase a cat or two, but a stern call, *You Jack,* from Obie, Sr. always found him quickly returning to the truck.

Some bullies decided to beat up Obie, Jr. during recess. They took his lunch and figured since his mother, Miss Lizzie, was a great cook, they would do the same thing each day. Leroy tried to help his brother, but the other boys were much bigger, and they began to take his lunch too.

Neither Leroy nor Obie, Jr. wanted to tell their folks what was going on at school. They were wrestling and tussling around with some friends when Obie, Jr. hollered like he was hurt. Immediately Jack rushed to the rescue and pinned down the boy who was wrestling with Obie, Jr. No matter how the boy struggled, Jack wasn't moving. Obie, Jr. was finally able to convince his dog that he was fine and Jack let their playmate get up. The

boys knew Jack was a great watchdog, but now they
realized just what a gold mine they had.

The next day, they all walked to school
together, and Jack returned to the wood yard for his
daily duties. The bullies took the boys lunches, but
this time; Leroy told them enough was enough. He
invited them out for a fight after school at an empty
lot they passed on the way home.

News of the fight was all over the school
and the last bell couldn't ring fast enough for Leroy
and Obie, Jr. They walked calmly out of the
schoolyard and started on their regular path home.
They were relieved to see Jack standing at his post.
He trotted toward them happily wagging his tail. A
crowd of curious kids followed the boys and Jack.
The two bullies had run ahead to get to the lot first.
They figured it would be short work to give the
boys their beating and get home for supper.

All of a sudden one of the bullies took a
swing at Obie, Jr., who fell to the ground and
howled like he was being skinned alive! Jack went
into action and knocked the bully to the ground,
placing all his shaggy weight squarely on top of the
surprised boy. Leroy and Obie, Jr. rushed forward

and began raining down fists and kicks on the parts of the bullies body that weren't covered by the thick blanket of dog fur. The crowd cheered and clapped as the bully begged for mercy! When the boys felt they had gotten a reasonable sense of satisfaction, Leroy called out, *You Jack,* and the obedient mutt quickly released his intended victim. The surprised boy bolted away like a streak of lightening! His friend wasn't about to suffer the same fate and had run away as soon as Jack had come forward. Leroy and Obie, Jr. took turns patting Jack on the head as they walked toward the wood yard.

News of the event in the empty lot easily and quickly reached the teacher. She was amused and secretly happy for Leroy and Obie, Jr. because she'd tried to stop the lunch beatings without any success. She was very concerned about Jack's involvement in the whole affair and decided a chat with Miss Lizzie was in order. As the teacher headed up Taylor Street, Leroy was the first to see her coming. He knew her presence meant trouble and he quickly found his brother to attempt to come up with a plan. They couldn't let the teacher get to their mother who was busy ironing in the back of the house.

Leroy and Obie, Jr. huddled at the edge of the back fence watching as the teacher opened the gate to enter the yard. As if on cue, Jack appeared from one end of the porch. When she attempted to walk up the steps, he began to snarl softly. *Come on Jack, you know me,* she pleaded. She tried to dodge the dog by moving to the other side of the step, but Jack quickly moved in the same direction, completely blocking her path to the porch. She called out for Miss Lizzie but couldn't be heard. The boys jumped with glee as their teacher decided not to argue with Jack and turned to leave the yard.

A few days later, the teacher happened upon Miss Lizzie in the A&P. She told her of the whole affair, beginning with the lunch beatings, the fight, and Jack's not letting her on the porch. They laughed at the boys' solution to the problem, but agreed it wasn't a good idea to encourage them to involve Jack in their battles.

When he heard the account of the proceedings, Obie, Sr. decided everyone involved would be punished, including Jack. As the leather strap was applied first to Leroy's bottom and then, to Obie, Jr., their father commanded Jack to appear from his hiding place under the porch. *You Jack,* Obie, Sr. called, and the dog slowly crept forward, keeping as low to the ground as he could. The boys nursed their own sore bottoms as they watched Jack get a few licks as just reward for his troubles. Obie, Sr. explained that Jack was doing what he was told when he held down the bully, but when he kept the teacher off the porch, he knew he was in the wrong. The boys were made to understand even though Jack was a wonderful playmate, his job was protecting the wood yard and they weren't to use him to fight their battles.

Jack knew his job and did it well. It was known by the locals that the dog loved everyone in the daytime, but wouldn't recognize Jesus himself at the wood yard after dark! Jack had a comfortable doghouse, but preferred to sleep on a pile of stacked wood right inside the fence. Anyone trying to enter the yard at night wouldn't be able to see Jack until it was much too late.

Obie, Sr. was known for his generosity. He'd been able to pull himself up by his own bootstraps and was willing to lend a hand to others in need. He allowed neighbors and friends credit when they needed it and sometimes gave kindling wood to elderly folks so they could cook and stay warm in winter.

No one paid much attention when a stranger appeared in the community. He purchased some wood and made friendly conversation as it was loaded. He remarked at Jack's friendly manner and patted him on the head. Over the weeks that passed, the man returned often to the wood yard, joining in on the chatter as people met each other coming and going. On each visit, the man would reach down and pet Jack. He even gave the boys some change to spend at the Chinese store. DeHeong was the community grocer and his clapboard store was a familiar site. The front entrance was lined with penny candy jars and the boys were all too happy to trade their money for Mary Jane's and jawbreakers.

Moses and Greater Young Zion Baptist Churches were only a few steps from each other. Between the end of Sunday school and the beginning of the main worship services, members

walked the few yards to DeHeong for pickled eggs,
pigs' feet, Cokes, cookies and gossip. The tiny
store would be packed with people, then thin out as
if by magic. The strains of the weekly processional
hymn, *We're Marching To Zion* would begin to
swell as folks littered the store counter with change
and stuffed their treats into purses and pockets to
quickly return to church.

The man who started out a stranger quickly
began to count himself as one of the regulars. He
could joke and laugh as loud as anyone and
everyone knew him. He decided the time was right
to make his move.

In the pitch-blackness of a chilly fall night,
he drove his truck as close to the wood yard as he
dared. He slid on a pair of work gloves and scouted
the outside of the fence for the best place to haul
himself over. He'd brought a soup bone for Jack
and figured while the dog was busy with the bone it
would be easy work to drop wood to the other side
of the fence. He'd load it in his truck and be on his
way, with no one being the wiser.

The man threw the bone into the wood yard
and since he didn't hear or see anything, figured the

coast was clear. Getting over the fence was no problem at all. He never saw what knocked him to the ground, but as he scrambled to get up, he felt a sharp pain in his rear end! Jack was shaking the seat of the man's britches like a shark determined to tear his prey apart! The man hollered the command he'd heard the family using. Over and over he screamed, *You Jack*, but the dog was strangely deaf and determined that the hide on the man's rear end was his for the taking.

Everyone in the house heard the ruckus and headed for the back door with Obie Sr. leading the pack. The confused man was still trying to reason with Jack, who'd turned into a fierce, growling hairball. Obie Sr. took his time and finally called out *You Jack*, and the obedient dog turned loose his grip and allowed the man to crumple into a painful heap. Jack presented himself at his master's feet for his pat on the head.

Jack don't know nobody at night, Mister, so you'd better get on out of here. The man was more than happy to comply and the family could only laugh when he dashed past them with the seat of his overhauls missing! *Back to bed, everybody*! Obie,

Sr. ordered. *There's work and school in the morning.* Wishing the excitement could have continued, the boys each patted Jack on the head as they passed by. Their father picked up the bone and with a laugh, threw the reward near Jack's sleeping place so there was no doubt it was alright for him to enjoy it.

Walker Baptist Institute

Emma Addie Douse read every single thing she could get her hands on. There were no public schools for colored people. Her father Warren and a lot of other people felt it was a waste of time for girls, especially Negroes, to get an education. They were expected to find husbands to take care of them while they nursed babies, cleaned, cooked and took care of white folks.

Rev. Dr. Charles Thomas Walker founded Walker Baptist Institute. Dr. Walker was also the minister of Tabernacle Baptist Church in Augusta. He'd become a very popular speaker and felt strongly about providing education for colored students. The school taught basic classes like math, science and grammar. There was also Latin and music. There was a fully equipped kitchen in the Home Economics Department and students cooked all kinds of foods. They learned how to manage any kind of kitchen duty. They even made candy for friends and family.

Emma had a maid's job that she went to early in the mornings. She fixed breakfast and lunch and got the family off to work and school. Then she took a trolley to Walker Baptist Institute. The people in charge gave her a special rate on tuition since her father Warren Douse was a member of the Ministers' Alliance that helped support the school. She spent every spare minute in the Home Economics Room. During lunchtime, Emma oiled sewing machines, and learned every kind of stitch that could be made. She also learned how to manage a household. At the end of the school day, she walked back to her job to cook the family's supper.

Young ladies who graduated from Walker Baptist Institute had to make everything they wore except their shoes! Hattie scrimped and saved and bought Emma a new pair for the graduation ceremony. Warren was as proud as a peacock!

This candy is good! It's really easy to make.

Walker Baptist Kisses

1 egg white	1/8 tsp. nutmeg
2 dashes salt	1/8 tsp. cloves
1/4 c. sugar	1 c. finely chopped
	pecans
1 tsp. Cinnamon	Pecan halves

Beat egg white with salt until stiff. Gradually beat in sugar mixed with spices. Fold in chopped pecans. Drop from teaspoon onto well-greased cookie sheet. Top with pecan halves. Bake at 250 degrees for 35 to 40 minutes. Makes about 2 dozen.

Tat….Tuck… Pleat

Tat… Tuck… Pleat.
You'd better make your stitches neat.
Fry the bacon crispy, and grits better hold the heat.
We won't sop lumpy gravy, with biscuits hard as sin.
Move a little quicker, we've got company coming in.

Tat…Tuck… Pleat.
It's time for the baby to eat.
He's still teething, so chew up his food.
Don't keep it in your mouth too long.
He cries when he's hungry and it makes my head ache.
Put a move on gal, for goodness sakes!

Tat…Tuck… Pleat.
Don't think of taking a seat.
Can colored folks ever be neat?
Can you do something but dance and sing?
Do we have to tell you every little thing?

Tat…Tuck… Pleat.
Go cook us something to eat.

Devine's Boy

Jim Washington was a sharp dresser and didn't mind spending the time it took to look good. He cleaned his felt hats with cornmeal and a stiff brush. He was the life of any party he went to, and could drink anyone under the table. He knew all about liquor. He'd out run every revenue agent in the Valley, making sure his Uncle Bo Jumper's moonshine got where it needed to go. Jim was the darling of the Devines. His mother Essie Bell left him with her Grandmother Harriet Devine when he was a baby. Essie had stars in her eyes for Daddy Grace and helped him start the United House of Prayer for All People. Momma Harriet thought Jim could do no wrong and let him have whatever he wanted. He grew up working in the fields for his Uncle Frank and surrounded by the love of the Devines.

All the folks in the Valley knew Devine's Boy, as he was called. As a teenager, he got a job in a textile mill where lots of Crackers were on the payroll. One night a rowdy bunch spotted Devine's Boy on his way home, and started shouting and calling him names. He was able to stay calm until one of the Crackers hit him in the face. They never knew what had hit them! Devine's Boy grabbed the one that passed the first lick and used him as a club to beat the others! Crackers went running every which way and he picked up one man and threw him through the plate glass window of the mill office! It didn't take long for a crowd to gather screaming for *the nigger's neck in a noose.* The night watchman, who knew Momma Harriet Devine, admitted the Crackers started the fight. After a few days, word got out that trouble was brewing. Devine's Boy decided he'd had enough and it was time for him and the Valley to part company. He headed for Philly to join the good times with the family that was already there.

Going Up North From Down South

Had enough of the South.
We're going up North.
We'll punch Jim Crow in the mouth.

We won't pick rice or cotton or beans,
but we'll still eat grits and collard greens.
We'll live in apartments and ride the subway.
We'll find better jobs with better pay.

It'll have to different any place that we find.
They'll give us respect and treat us kind.
We'll look in the eyes of whomever we greet.
No "colored only" signs; no bus back seats.

Had enough of the South. We're already up North.
It's different here you can bet.
There's no wide-open spaces or familiar faces.
We might have a bit of regret.

We came up North from down South.
We saw some different sites.
We waited tables and worked in hotels.
We still answer the bell, and far as we can tell.
We haven't gained any new rights.

Wherever we are and wherever we roam.
Be it far away or close to home.
A better life hopefully our children will see.
The place where we live will be where we feel free.

The Pigpen

Jim met Emma and they both loved to dance.
The Pigpen was their favorite place.
There was heat from a barrel in the middle of the
floor,
And certainly not much space.

The smell in the room was an odd perfume of
Fried chicken and beer from the bar.
The folks jumped and bumped.
The music was loud.
They came from near and far.

The joint sat low in a hollow pit.
The Pigpen lived up to its name.
It looked like an outhouse, but nobody cared.
They partied just the same.

Hop in the wagon and hitch up the mule!
Drop the mullet fish in the hot grease.
Colored folks work daily from kink to kink.
On Friday they need some release.

Emma's hair was all pressed and waved.
For weeks their extra change they saved.
Jim and Emma got hitched by the Justice of Peace.
Jim's suit pants had quite a crease.

To the Pigpen they did invite friends and kin.
Wasn't enough room for them all to get in.
They partied till the sun traded places with the
moon.
Nobody dared to leave the joint too soon.

Time marches on and nothing stays the same.
Jim's now a nephew of his Uncle Sam.
He's a soldier at Fort Gordon, a potato peeler in
his hand.
Mr. Truman shipped him off to a foreign land.

Emma wears her hair in a Victory Roll.
Everything's in short supply.
The Pigpen still jumps, now with soldiers on pass.
Everyone hopes the war won't last.

Colored boys you turned in your broom for a gun.
You're far from the Pigpen with no place to run.
Jump in the foxhole, the white boys won't mind.
They haven't put out the "whites only" sign.

There's no smell of beer or chicken or fish.
Everybody present has got just one wish.
They pray hard to the One up above,
"Let me get back to the ones I love!"

If you visit the Pigpen, there'll be a crowd outdoors.
You'll see plenty dirt 'cause there ain't no floors.
Bring your woman and wrap your liquor in a brown
paper sack.
If you show up once, you're bound to come back.

Miss Thelma and Miss Emma

Miss Thelma and Miss Emma shop together on Broad
Street.
They say" Hello" to all they meet.
Miss Thelma is light and can pass for white.
The two of them make quite a site.

A beautiful lady and her colored maid
Are out on the town for a stroll.
No one knows the two are best pals,
And enjoying playing the role.

The war is on and many things are
In really short supply.
It's a well known fact when there's any to be had,
White customers only can buy.

Toilet paper and soap were sold out if you were brown..
"Sorry missy", the clerk would say with a frown.
For white customers the clerk would smile and look
around.
"It's under the counter, I'm sure it can be found."

Miss Thelma and Miss Emma knew the routine well.
They knew what they could buy
And what the clerks would sell.

Miss Emma would wait in an alley out back,
And send Miss Thelma inside.
She'd put on white gloves and a scarf on her head.
Any signs of her true race she'd hide.

Miss Thelma would go up to a rather young clerk,
And whisper in a sweet little voice.
"Is there any toilet paper or soap today?
I know you have no choice.

You must keep these things hidden under counters and
shelves.
Or we that are white would have none for ourselves.
I'll take two rolls of paper and two bars of soap.
This war will end quickly, I certainly hope!"

"Thanks so much, Madame,
And do come again"
Miss Thelma would smile at her newfound friend.
Then she'd turn and walk out the front door,
To try it again at another store.

She'd run down the alley to her friend she'd call,

"Look Nanaw, the niggers didn't get it all!"

The two ladies would whoop and grin and laugh!

Then they'd split their loot in half.

Miss Thelma and Miss Emma shop together on Broad

Street.

No two smarter ladies will you ever meet!

<u>One Way Only</u>

Momma loves to tell people about her trip to the hospital on the day I was born and how I managed to stop traffic even before I got here!

Our cousin Albert and his sister Lillie ran a produce market on the first floor of the building they owned at 351 Christian Street in Philadelphia. My Great Aunt Geneva and her husband Johnnie lived on the second floor and my parents were upstairs.

Momma was pregnant, but everyone agrees that my Daddy carried me. He had all the symptoms and discomfort; swollen feet and ankles, morning sickness, rashes, hemorrhoids, and cravings for foods he didn't even like. As Momma gained weight, Daddy withered away.

He couldn't get along with anyone and when he walked down the street, folks stepped to one side, like Moses parting the Red Sea. Momma said they took a walk one afternoon and passed by some men playing checkers. It was just a few weeks before I was born and she looked like she was pushing her own wheelbarrow. An elderly man looked up from the checkerboard and said, *Well, it won't be long now!*

My Daddy turned into a human tornado! The checkerboard went sailing through the air and everyone scrambled to get out of harm's way. He grabbed the man and was about to pound him into the pavement when everyone heard a loud, high pitched screech. *Let that man alone, Jim! He didn't mean nothing!* Dad stopped long enough to notice Miss Betty, the lady who ran the local liquor house. She'd been leaning out of her upstairs window watching the street below. Momma liked to say that Betty was a heavy-set, light-skinned woman who could get peace out of confusion. She came downstairs in a flash and gathered up my folks like a mother hen overseeing her chicks. She led them toward her apartment building, telling everyone peeping around the corner that the show was over for the day. The old man moaned that he didn't mean nothing and he thought Momma looked pretty *in the family way.* Betty, the perfect mother hen, shushed him softly and gently herded my father into the building, patting his shoulder and making soft clucking noises as she nodded her head.

My Daddy obeyed and moved toward the apartment, looking over his shoulder for anyone else he could pick on for any reason. The whole neighborhood was on notice that Jim Washington, *Pregnant Daddy*, was not to be messed with.

Early in the morning on the day I was born, Momma made the trip to Hannemanns Hospital. It wasn't time for me to arrive, and everyone, including Grandma Hattie, who'd just come in on the train from Augusta, was sent back to Christian Street. Aunt Geneva was fit be tied! Even though she'd never had any children of her own, she was convinced the hospital staff didn't know what they were doing. When Momma's pains became closer together that same morning, Geneva said her, *I told you so's*, loud enough for the whole neighborhood to hear and ordered everyone to Uncle Johnny's car for yet another trip to the hospital.

Uncle Johnny had worked as a chauffeur, driving all over the country. In the section of Philly where my family lived, every other street was one-way. My nervous uncle ignored a sign and with both hands fixed to the steering wheel, puttered forward, in the wrong direction, like a horse with blinders on. A policeman happened to be on hand, and Aunt Geneva rolled her window down and shouted, W*e've got a lady in here fixing to have a baby!* The policeman figured out the route he thought Uncle Johnny was trying to take and stopped the traffic that could have ended my entrance before I'd gotten a chance to make it! On the empty street, Uncle Johnny drove up to the hospital like the professional chauffeur he used to be. When the cop saw Momma trying to lift herself out of the car, he got a nurse who brought a wheel chair. *Is this your first grandchild, Pops?* My Uncle nodded his head, *Yassuh!* *Well,* continued the policeman, *the next time you come to the hospital, please pay attention to the one-way signs. You could get somebody killed*! Uncle Johnny gave him another firm *Yassuh,* just as Aunt Geneva snatched him inside.

My Daddy told everyone who would listen that he knew the minute I was born. At exactly 11:45 a.m., he was sitting on a pile of hides at the tannery where he worked. He said he felt like someone took a weight off his shoulders.

I came into the world on July 17, 1952 with red cheeks, pink lips and beauty marks. Momma nicknamed me *The Madame* because she thought I looked like the lady of some grand manor house. Instead of closing my hands in tight fists, my long fingers were wide open. I looked as if I was constantly waving *Hello* to everyone! Grandma Essie declared it was all the devil's doing because I didn't look like any normal baby.

Our cousins Albert and Lillie had never been around any infants and both were scared to death of the squirming, screaming little bundle Momma brought into their building. I had a big bandage around my middle to hold the silver dollar that kept my belly button from poking out. (Momma had seen many babies at the nursery school with huge navels and she was determined mine was going to be an *inny* instead of an *outty*). Lillie finally got used to changing diapers and found I wasn't as fragile as I looked.

The Christian Street neighborhood was filled with all kinds of people. A Jewish family owned the deli a few doors away. When I refused the pretty pacifier Aunt Geneva bought for me, the wife of the storeowner solved the problem. Each day I was given a fresh bagel tied with a string around my neck! Momma admits that by evening, it didn't look too good, riddled with tiny bullet-like holes from my new teeth, but it was just what the doctor ordered to soothe the itch of teething. Everyone delighted in spoiling me and I was, as Momma says, *Rotten to the Corps and good to the Navy!*

Abide With Me

In January of 1953, Jim Washington was on his way to work on an icy road in Franklin Township, Pennsylvania. The car hit a patch of ice, and spun around so that another car plowed into the back seat on the side where my Dad was sitting. Grandma told me he was a friend to the last because he allowed all the other men to be taken to the hospital first. Some of them had cuts and bruises that looked more serious and he didn't look hurt at all. By the time the ambulance returned, he'd died of a punctured lung.

Momma gets sad when she talks about my father. He loved to dress nice and had a great smile. I was confused when she said he'd never come home from the war. (That didn't make sense because he had to be around when I was born). Momma explained that she really didn't know my father after World War II, so as far as she was concerned the real Jim Washington died on the beach at Iwo Jima. He talked about that battle and living in a foxhole for eight weeks. His best buddy was blown to bits when he picked up a strange-looking dagger. My Dad told about the island being surrounded by boiling water and crawling with Japanese soldiers, who'd dug into the rock. The man who came back from that nightmare, screamed in his sleep, and went crazy when there was thunder and lightening. Momma has a cut on her arm from when my Dad tried to drag her under their bed during a storm. She told me he kept screaming for her to take cover.

Momma was so disgusted with my Dad's behavior that she tried to give him back to the army. She found a veteran's hospital in Alabama willing to help him get used to not being a soldier. By the time he'd decided it was a good idea, he was killed in the auto accident.

I wish my Dad had stayed around long enough for me to get to know him. He must have loved me a lot because according to everyone around, he was with me for years after his death. Grandma calls *Abide With Me*, Jim's hymn.

Momma had a hard time keeping sitters for me. When we were still in Philly, she got a job near Market Street. She'd asked our Cousin Albert to keep me, but he said he was too busy with the produce and fish market he ran on the first floor of the building. Momma was happy to find a lady with a nice apartment who said she'd be glad to have the job. We were coming down the stairs when Albert ran toward the landing, pale and out of breath. *Leave me alone!* He shouted, as his arms waved at someone or something Momma couldn't see. *I'll do it! Do what?* Momma asked him, but Albert wasn't listening or talking to her. Albert grabbed me, snatched up my things and headed for the store. When Momma tried to say something he told her to go to work and not look back.

Even Grandma Hattie tells a story about my Dad hanging around me. She adored my father from the first time they met and was proud of the fact that he told people she was his mother! (He told Momma she could have Grandma Essie instead).

Momma worked at the USO and had to stay late to finish a float for the Christmas parade. Grandma was keeping me and heard a noise on the porch. She went outside to look, but didn't see anything. When she stepped back into the bedroom, I was sitting on the bed playing pat-a-cake with the air! That wouldn't have been all that bad, but Grandma saw the mattress sink and then rise like someone had gotten up off the bed. She said she was scared for a minute, but got a comfortable feeling that everything was all right. *I'm here now, Jim,* Grandma spoke out loudly. I pointed to the door, turned my head to one side and said, *There goes that man!* I don't remember any of that, but if Grandma Hattie said it happened, it did.

In the produce market, Albert fixed my playpen near the window so I could reach some of the fruits and vegetables. I put my tiny teeth prints in a bunch of them that he sold to customers who thought I was cute. They would come over and kiss me and that drove my cousin nearly nuts! He got coleslaw from the neighborhood deli and doctored it with loads of chopped garlic. We had hot dogs for lunch and it wasn't long before customers started blowing me kisses from across the room! When Momma got home from work, Albert hadn't had a chance to change my diaper, so my perfume hit her from both ends! After a chat with Momma, the deli refused to sell Albert any coleslaw.

Great Gumbo!

I've always had a hard time sitting still and I made life in the produce market very difficult. When I got too big for the playpen, Momma came up with a plan to keep me safe and out of the way. She put a pallet under a table with all my favorite toys. A leather harness went around my shoulders and back and the leash end was tied to the table leg. My Great Aunt Geneva, Grandma Essie's sister had a fit when she came home and found me in such a fix. Aunt Geneva has always had a quick temper and can out cuss any sailor! Momma and Lillie didn't say anything when my Aunt untied me and headed to her apartment on the second floor. *Ya'll ought to be ashamed, tying this baby out like some poor little cow.* She called them some names I'm not allowed to say and went on to tell them, *Ya'll are only treating her like this because she doesn't have a daddy to look out for her!* Momma said she gave Lillie a wink and they decided to go shopping the next Saturday.

Aunt Geneva agreed to keep me and swore she wasn't going to use the harness because I wasn't that bad. She invited her friend Mary to help in the store and Momma and Lillie took off to Market Street. Miss Mary loved to play cards and visit with the customers. Her laugh could be heard on the next corner! She and Geneva got busy in the store and I got busy too. There were fish to be cleaned so I got up on a soapbox to reach the table. The box tipped over and I fell in a big bucket of Pine Sol and water. I didn't smell too good and Aunt Geneva had to walk up to the third floor to give me a bath and change my clothes.

Back downstairs in the market, Auntie was determined to rock me to sleep, but I get seasick easily, so I threw up in her lap and wiggled away. She climbed the stairs again to change her clothes, leaving me with Mary.

Albert had gotten a bushel basket of okra and while Mary whooped it up with customers, I filled the basket with sawdust from the floor under the fish-cleaning table. I stirred it up with my hands and it would have probably made great gumbo, but I didn't get the chance to find out.

When Momma and Lillie returned, Mary and Aunt Geneva had finished wiping sawdust from the prickly okra pods, one at a time. My Aunt had her dress rolled up in the front with her feet in a pan of water. She and Mary were laughing and playing spades. I was sleeping peacefully on my pallet, snugly harnessed to the table leg.

Okra Pickles

2 lbs. Small whole okra

3 cups white vinegar

1 cup water

2 tbsp. Pickling salt

2 tsp. Hot pepper sauce (Only if you like your pickles hot)

Put these spices in each jar:

1/4 tsp. Dill seed

1/8 tsp. Mustard seed

1 clove garlic

Wash okra and soak in cold water at least for an hour.

Sterilize jars and mix the brine.

Brine: Put the vinegar, pickling salt and water in a pot and simmer for about 10 minutes.

(Add the pepper sauce if you're making hot pickles).

Put the spices and garlic in the jars.

Pack in the okra tightly. (It works great if you put one pod up and one down.)

Pour the hot brine over the okra and leave ?" room
at the top.

Push the air out of the jars with something that's not
metal. Be careful not to poke the okra.

Put seals and rings on the jars and boil them in a
pot. Make sure the water covers the whole jar.

Boil them for 10 minutes after the water starts to
roll.

Cool jars and hide them for about 2 weeks. (That's
the hardest part).

Who I Am

Ham hocks, okra, butterbeans, rice.
I won't mind if you serve me twice.
Cornbread, biscuits, rolls and jam,
"Loves to eat" that's who I am.

Puddin, pie, chocolate cake layers high,
No special diet for me.
Dip my meat in gravy.
Say the blessing and pass the plate.
Please don't call me to the table late!

Ham hocks, okra, butterbeans, rice.
I won't mind at all if you serve me twice!

The Visit

When it's really hot, I like to lie on the living room floor in front of the fan in the window. We spend a lot of time sitting on the big cement porch that wraps around our house. My favorite time is early evening when the sun is about to go down. Mr. Jackson puts wet rags in a barrel in the driveway, and lights them on fire. The smoke keeps the *gallon-nippers* away. One nip from one of those mosquitoes and they take a gallon of your blood!

Momma's been complaining about our worn out porch furniture. She painted the metal and made some new cushions but it still looked pretty tired. We were all outside helping Grandma plant a new blue hydrangea bush, when I looked up and saw a funny, slow moving truck in the curve. There were all kinds of beads hanging from the rear-view mirror, and it had a cover like a huge turtle shell. The whole thing creaked, groaned and rattled as it moved. We couldn't take our eyes off it and our feet moved us closer to the fence for a better look. Grandma said we were about to get a visit from the Gypsies.

I'd heard stories about Gypsies snatching
kids away from their families and selling them, so I
ducked behind my Momma. The thing at our gate
looked like *Mother Hubbard's Shoe* in a bad dream,
and I was sure there had to be kids tied up in there.
Momma told me I didn't have a thing to worry
about because if they did kidnap me, I'd be brought
home fast as lightening after I'd asked a million
questions and ate up all their groceries!

The driver stuck his head out the window
and asked if we'd be interested in buying some
hand-made porch furniture. He had a big beautiful
smile and black wavy hair. There was furniture
piled on the back as high as it could go, lashed on
with ropes that wound around everything. I was
still clinging to Momma when she stepped forward
and said she'd look at the furniture.

As the man turned the engine off, it gave a
gasp and a loud thud. He was out of the truck in a
flash. There was a pretty young woman in the front
seat, who sprang out and came around the front of
the truck. Her eyes lit up as she took notice of the
pink climbing roses all over the fence. She walked
forward, never taking her eyes off the blooms. She

nearly stumbled into the fence as she touched one of the small pink flowers and bent down to take a long sniff of the scent. I tried not to stare, but it was hard to take my eyes off someone so excited about a rose.

Grandma Hattie nodded her head at the lady, who quickly plucked a bloom and held it in both hands for another deep smell. The lady disappeared around the side of the truck and came back with an older lady, who must have been somewhere under the pile of furniture. They went to the fence, and Grandma said they could have all the roses they wanted. They smiled and nodded as they filled their pockets with flowers.

Momma decided to buy some furniture, so I went into the house for her purse. When I came back outside, Gypsies were all over the place! There were two children; a boy and a girl, whose big eyes darted around quickly. They looked glad to get out for a while and I was still trying to figure out how they all got in to start with.

As the man put the furniture on the porch, the ladies raved about the roses. Grandma asked if they'd like a cool drink of water. The family of

Gypsies couldn't have been happier if they'd been asked to stay for supper!

Grandma went into the house, and I followed. She got a tray and our pretty blue glasses with the ships on them. (Granddad got a free glass each time he filled the car with gas. He doesn't bring home many presents, so the blue glasses are very special to Grandma). She filled the tulip pitcher with ice, even though the well water comes out of the tap cold enough to frost the glasses. We filled a plate with Murray's Butter Cookies. Murray Biscuit Company is across the street from Auntie Annie's house on Taylor Street, and her husband Jessie and brother, Obie, Jr. have worked there for years. Taylor Street smells like coconut bars or butter cookies and there's always plenty for any occasion.

Grandma put the pitcher and glasses on the tray with napkins. We carried it all to the porch and she began to pour the water. The glasses disappeared off the tray like magic! The man with the wavy hair emptied his glass faster than I've ever seen anyone drink before. I went in the house for two more pitchers of water! Grandma presided over the pitcher, glasses and cookies like she was serving a full course meal. She didn't even blink as the Gypsies gulped down the water and cookies like a Thanksgiving feast. *Drink all you want!* Grandma chirped, *It's the best tasting water in Richmond County.* No one's glass stayed empty long, and it was hard to hear anything over the gulping and slurping noises. Even the flies and mosquitoes hung in the air while the Gypsies feasted. There wasn't an extra crumb of cookie or drop of water left.

It was getting late when Mr. Jackson came out and fired up the smoke barrel. Some of our neighbors came to see our new furniture and everyone relaxed around the yard and porch. Grandma gave the older Gypsy lady cuttings of her new hydrangea bush, with the roots wrapped in a wet napkin. Momma told the women if they named the cutting Hattie, after my Grandma, it would grow twice as big. Everybody laughed as the Gypsies headed toward their funny looking house-on-wheels.

As Momma handed the man the money for the furniture, he looked in his hand and tried to give some of it back. She refused to take it and offered her hand for the man to shake. He reached out, pulled Momma toward him and gave her a big hug.

Everyone went around the side of the truck and melted in. We waved and the pretty lady held on to her flowers like some kind of special treasure. I watched the truck go around the curve and out of sight.

Every time I sit in the furniture, I try to picture a Gypsy camp with people making furniture, laughing, and maybe even dancing. I told Grandma I liked our water, but I'd never spent a lot of time thinking about it. We have so many cookies, we get tired of eating them and Momma keeps telling me we have much to be grateful for.

The big blue hydrangea at the corner of our porch helps me remember that somewhere there's another one named Hattie in the company of some people who helped us be more grateful for some of the things we take for granted.

Butter cookies from Murray's taste fine, but these are much better!

Butter Cookies

2 sticks of butter

1 cup of sugar

3 1/2 cups flour

2 tsp. Vanilla

Mix butter until light and fluffy. Add in the sugar and mix well. Add flour a little at a time, mixing well after each addition. Add vanilla. After all the ingredients are mixed roll the dough into golf ball sized pieces. Place two inches apart on an ungreased cookie sheet.

Dip a fork into sugar and make criss-cross lines. Bake in a 300 degree oven on the top rack for 25-30 minutes or until edges are a light brown color.

(Make sure you have some cold milk to go with them).

Plea To Bee

Mr. Bee, Please be nice to me and make some honey
in this jar.
I put in all your favorite stuff, but it must not be
enough.
'Cause all I've heard is buzzing so far.

Mr. Bee, please be nice to me and make honey quick
as you can.
Grandma's biscuits are almost done.
I can smell them baking in the pan.
The butter's been churned, the tables been set.
Mr. Bee won't you be a good pet?

Mr. Bee, please be nice to me.
You're not happy and I don't have a clue.
I put in fresh clover, some flowers and dew.
Now, Mr. Bee it's all up to you.

Hot biscuits with honey would sure be grand.
But I won't complain if I have to eat jam.
Mr. Bee, please be nice to me.

The Search

I'm having a really hard time finding God. I've looked everywhere I can think of, but I'm not having any luck. Since Granddad is a preacher, I thought he'd be able to help me. When I asked him where I'd find God, he said, *God is everywhere.* (Granddad's got a limp, but he can move fast when he thinks I might ask him a hard question). I turned around and he was gone.

I asked Grandma where I'd find God and she told me I needed to be still and listen because God was in the wind and everything around me. I closed the doors, turned off the lights and sat in the living room. I closed my eyes and listened real hard. I thought I'd hear a booming voice calling my name but all I heard was crickets, and Granddad snoring in the other room.

Nuns have to know about God. After all, they're married to Jesus. Father Sheehan says the nuns are the Brides of Christ. The Sisters of Saint Francis of Assisi teach at Immaculate Conception Academy, where I go to school. They live in a big brick house across from Mrs. Luvenia Pearson's

School of Beauty on Twelfth Street. My Granddad had a fit when Momma decided to send me to the Catholic school, but Momma told him she had to work all the time and the nuns only had to pray and teach. I could go to public school if he'd stay home and help me with my lessons. Granddad never mentioned anything about school again.

My first grade teacher, Sister Mary Rita was very pretty with freckles and wispy pieces of red hair coming out from under her habit. Sometimes it was hard to understand what she was saying but Momma told me I had to try harder to listen because she was from Ireland and they all talked funny. Sister Mary Rita made the long trip to this country on a boat, because I heard Momma say she'd just gotten off of it. She wasn't old and wrinkled like most of the other nuns and I liked her a lot.

It must be hard being married to Jesus. You have to wear so many clothes! My cousin Sandra and I go to the convent for piano lessons and out back there's a clothesline with under things on it. They aren't like the panties we wear, but Momma says the nuns aren't allowed to be in fashion at all.

Sandra's mother Ellen is Grandma Hattie's niece. Ellen's father Obie, Sr., is Grandma's oldest brother. Cousin Ellen, her husband John, and their children, Sandra and Sylvia live over on Steiner Avenue, not too far from Wooten Road. Sandra's grandmother, Cousin John's mother, lives with them also. Gran doesn't hear too well but she makes sure everyone eats their oatmeal. Cousin Ellen is a nurse and works in the operating room. Cousin John is a chef at the same Veteran's Hospital and works on a later shift, so he takes us to school in the mornings and Momma brings us home. The Wilsons are family friends and Sammy and Rosemary ride with us. Sometimes Mr. Wilson takes us to school. He thinks the streets are his own personal racetracks and I've seen more than one person scrambling to get out of his way! We nicknamed one of the streets on our route, *Dodge City!* It was anybody's guess who had to dodge whom when we went through there with Mr. Wilson at the wheel.

Sister Mary Reginald always has a smile on her face and I like her. The day I went up to her, everyone was on the schoolyard for recess. She

smiled when she saw me. *Hello Jamersinz! How
are you this fine day?* I managed to blurt out that I
was fine. I don't like being called Jamersinz, but it's
the name Momma gave me. Nobody says it right
and I see it spelled wrong so much, sometimes I
forget how to spell it myself. At home I'm called
Jimmy and most kids call me Jamesina or
something like that. I prefer to be called Jayme, but
I answer to most anything that sounds close.

Sister Mary Reginald asked me about
Momma and my piano lessons with Sister Mary
Albee. Somehow I couldn't get the words out to
ask her anything about God. Maybe Grandma was
right and I just had to listen harder. Maybe God is a
woman and upset because people keep calling Her
Him. She might be strong and smart like Momma,
but I still don't understand why she isn't talking to
me. I wonder if I've given Her a headache with so
many questions? (Granddad says that wherever I
am, there'd better be a supply of Goody Powders).

The people in Granddad's churches shout
jump around and faint on Sunday. They say God
makes them feel happy. I've gotten close to some

of them and I don't think happiness from God smells like Grandma's peach brandy.

How can whatever God has to tell me be important if I can't hear or see it? Momma calls me an imp sometimes and says I act like one of the devil's minions. Granddad tells me it's up to the devil's imps to get people to do bad things. I've stirred up a few anthills and chunked a rock or two, but ever so often, Granddad checks my head for horns. Maybe that's the reason I can't hear what God is trying to tell me! My horns are in the way and I can only hear messages from the devil.

I heard that when people are possessed by demons, they scream, talk in other voices and do horrible things. I asked Granddad if he thought I was possessed, and he said any demon that got into me was in serious trouble. Now, I'm really worried about missing whatever God has to say to me.

I think that smart people are closer to God. Both Momma and Granddad have an extra roll of flesh at the base of their skulls. It's called a *knowledge knot* and some folks believe it holds extra brains. I check my skull for a knot all the time. If I could fill up my head with lots of stuff, maybe I'd have an easier time finding God.

Miss Ollie Small told us in Sunday school that we could find God in the Bible. We have to say a scripture for memory and it can't be *Jesus wept.* One kid tried that and Miss Ollie really laid into him.

Miss Ollie Small isn't small! She's light enough to pass for white and must be the biggest lady I've ever seen! She isn't fat either. Her chest is at least fifty inches across and when she folds her arms she looks like the big hunk of rock on the insurance commercials. Grandma says Miss Ollie's father was German. (If that's what Germans look like, it's no wonder Mr. Truman sent the colored soldiers to help win World War II). Miss Ollie wears her jet-black hair parted in the middle and pulled back in a tight bun. I've never been to a prison, but I imagine the warden would look like Miss Ollie.

I love going to the Wallace Branch Library! Mrs. Addie Powell is in charge and she shows films and points out interesting books. She even has contests to see who can read the most books in the fastest time. I checked out one about opera and Miss Ollie was on the cover! (If it wasn't Miss Ollie, the lady looked exactly like her). I wondered if she had a costume with a helmet with horns, a brass brassier and a spear. Momma said if she did, Miss Small wouldn't wear it to Sunday school. Miss Ollie might know where God is, but I'm too scared to ask her.

I listen hard in church for signs of God, but it gets so noisy, I can't hear anything. Momma tells me I can't hear what's being said if I'm talking myself. I wonder how anybody can hear what the preacher is saying because they're all chattering back at once. I suppose God must talk to the preacher the night before when it's quiet. I don't know when the other people hear their message.

When Granddad is going to preach, he starts out looking neat and pressed. Grandma Hattie irons his shirts on Saturday afternoons with so much starch they could stand by themselves. Granddad pulls up the sleeves and puts armbands on. Momma keeps telling him armbands went out with high-buttoned shoes, but he doesn't listen. I guess he just wants to feel his own skin in his shirt. Since he doesn't have to iron, Granddad has no problem coming home with wrinkles.

It doesn't take much for most folks in the church to get worked up. Some start out moaning or singing softly to themselves, but as the preacher gets louder, so do they. White preachers just stand in the pulpit and read their sermons. They don't jump, hop or bounce around, so they don't go home with wrinkled shirts. (That's probably why they get out of church much sooner than we do). Momma says the richer the church, the stiffer the preacher is. As the pockets get emptier, the preachers get looser. (I'd think the rich people would have more to shout about, but it's the poor folks with all the moves).

The Reverend H. L. Harrison at Greater Young Zion Missionary Baptist Church moves more than any preacher I've ever seen. (His pockets must be very empty). He reads the scripture quietly and gives his text more than once, like he might be proud he really does have one. He talks for a while and no one says too much, except Deacon Robert Conley. He talks back to any preacher in the pulpit. *Oh come on now, Rev! You ain't telling 'em loud enough! Tell 'em agin! They didn't hear you!* Any preacher that can go a few rounds with Deacon Conley can get through anything.

Harrison heats up quickly, yelling in grunts and sounding like something's caught in his throat. He pulls out a big white hanky to sop up the water that pours down his face and neck. Momma says he sweats because he drinks a lot. I just thought they meant he drank a lot of water until I heard her and Grandma whispering about how he always smells like liquor, but the congregation loves the shows he puts on.

I decided it might be easier for God to speak to me if I was baptized. During a revival meeting, I sat on the mourner's bench. When the invitational hymn started and the chairs were put in the front of the church, I sat in one. I answered the questions Rev. Harrison asked about believing in Jesus and I joined the group of candidates waiting to be baptized.

I like to swim, and love water, but I was a bit nervous about the whole thing. On that baptism Sunday I put on the white robe Momma made for me, and my hair was wrapped in a towel. I stood in line in the small room on the side of the church where all the ministers put on their robes. The baptismal pool is under the pulpit and the floorboards were taken up and leaned to one side. I could hear water gushing into the waist high space. When it was full, Harrison waded in with another deacon. Both of them were wearing hip boots and I was really scared!

The congregation was singing *Take Me To The Water*, without any piano playing. I closed my eyes and tried to think about swimming at Jones pool, near Bethlehem Community Center where we have Girl Scout meetings. The person in front of me disappeared down the steps and I held my breath. When it was my turn, I stepped forward and the deacon in the pool took my hand and guided me in. People were crowded around trying to get a good view. The deacon that helped me into the pool folded my hands over my chest and I felt my heart beating like a drum. I knew everyone could hear it too. I also knew God was waiting to speak to me as soon as I came up out of the water. Rev. Harrison put his hands on top of mine and just before he pulled me backward into the water, I smelled his breath. As the water covered my face, I heard him say, *A little deeper Deacon,* and more water rushed over me. I was certain I was about to be drowned! Just then the deacon helped Harrison pull me up. The robe had stuck to my skin and water was coming out of my nose. I wanted to scream and I knew it wasn't God talking to me. It had to be the devil because the voice was telling me to hit the preacher in the jaw!

My ears were ringing and I couldn't hear much of anything. There wasn't any booming voice and I didn't feel the need to go stiff and pass out. As my friend Hattie Mae Mobley helped me get into dry clothes, I could hardly believe God still hadn't bothered to say anything to me after everything I'd just gone through.

Rev. H.L. Harrison is very tall and thin with a pleasant smile, and in the pulpit he acts like a spring that's been wound tight as it can go. Like a carnival ride, he spins around waving his hankie in his hand, leaping into the air taking the hearts of the women members with him. By the time he's completely fired up, over half the church is standing, but Harrison's feet never touch the floor. He floats above the noise saying the same words over and over. *Ain't God good? Have you tried Him?* The congregation screams *Amen!* I want to scream too, but I can't get up the nerve. I want everyone to be quiet so I can hear whatever God has to tell me. If He's anywhere around, I'm sure He must be deaf from all the noise.

I've noticed that some people manage to keep still while Harrison puts on his show. Deacon Ike Eubanks is chairman of the deacon board and he's a very nice man. (I wish he wouldn't call me *Little Hattie* the way he does. I guess he thinks I look like Grandma. I don't think so). I still like Deacon Ike. He never jumps around or falls out during the service. His wife Sadie is a beautician and is president of the Deaconess board. Sadie Eubanks works at the Augusta National for Mrs. Eisenhower when she and President Ike come to town. Sometimes, Miss Sadie cries during the sermon, but she sits still. Momma and Grandma never move.

Mrs. Lou Bryant is another story. She's a short, stocky browned-skinned woman who wears the most stylish hats. She has a crooked knee and walks with a limp, but she knows how to look good.

Her hats have fruit, flowers, feathers or birds and sometimes all four, on them. One time you couldn't see Miss Lou's face under a load of hat with plastic grapes trailing off the side. It looked good enough to eat!

When Miss Lou is about to go stiff, she starts saying the word *Yes,* over and over again. She gets louder and louder as the *S* sound on the end of the word grows longer and longer. It begins to sound like a snake hissing. By the time Miss Lou starts to weave back and forth, big drops of sweat roll down her face along with her pancake powder.

Ushers in white uniforms with hankies up their sleeves begin a processional to the pew where she sits. Almost like a dance, someone removes the hat from her head and hands it to someone else in the congregation. Another usher takes her glasses off and Miss Lou stands up and begins fanning her arms in and out, and in and out. The arm waving follows the rhythm of the music and I've seen her hit new ushers in the face when they've gotten in the way. The rest of Miss Lou's painted face slides down her neck as ushers try to mop up the sweat. Her eyes roll back in her head and Miss Lou falls backward, stiff as a board! Ushers calmly carry her towards the swinging double doors at the back of the church and the gates open wide for the whole church to start falling out. Not one performance holds a candle to Miss Lou, but as the numbers swell, Harrison cranks up his voice and leaps that much higher.

I practice my stiff fainting in the backyard. I know I'm going to hear God's voice telling me to fall out and I want to be ready. I feel good walking around the yard looking at the trees and birds. It's fun watching the ducks fill the water cans with pebbles, and I chase the turkeys just to see them run. I love it when Momma lets me put the sprinkler on the hose and I get to jump around in the water! I can play for hours! I don't care who sees me and if I could get away with it, I'd take off my clothes and run around naked. I think I'm supposed to feel the same way in church. That must be the spirit everyone is talking about. Maybe being touched by God is just being happy to be alive.

My Granddad ends his sermon with a song. It's strange how he can sing after all that yelling. I can understand why people would be very happy listening to his mellow tenor voice. The part I think should be the happiest seems sad to the rest of the people. As Granddad sings, people all over the church cry and slowly put themselves back into some kind of order. Harrison doesn't sing that well, but someone else starts up a hymn while he slumps into the big pulpit chair.

Grandma says God sees everything, so I'm sure He knows I've been trying to understand whatever message He's trying to give me. I'm going to keep practicing my stiff faint just in case the spirit touches me someplace other than my backyard.

Miss Ollie Small

Miss Ollie Small isn't small at all.
She must be at least six feet tall.
She's as wide across as a mule or a horse.
Rarely does she smile.

At Sunday school she puts up with no fuss.
She scares the tar right out of us!
If you don't learn your Bible verse,
You might as well go and call the hearse!

Miss Ollie is straight as an arrow is she,
And teaches us how we ought to be.
You don't chew gum or whisper or grin,
If her Primary Class you want to stay in.

You open the Good Book and close your mouth.
We're the best-behaved class anywhere in the
South.

Miss Ollie loves us and we know that's a fact.
Like ladies and gents she wants us to act.

She sets good example.
We follow her lead.
We listen to her lessons.
On each word we feed.

If you want to learn the Bible, Miss Ollie's the one.
You'll have to sit still.
It might even be fun!

Miss Sadie's New Hat

Miss Sadie's got a new hat, fancy that.
Miss Mamie had more than she could wear.
They arrive by mail and even by rail.
The two ladies make quite a pair.

Miss Sadie does hair and fixes it fine,
She works at Augusta National sometimes.
Miss Sadie's husband's name is Ike.
He works at the Richmond Hotel.
Ike's uniform has gold trim on his sleeve.
He's in charge of the bellhops, I believe.

Miss Mamie's Ike is the President.
He plays golf on the Masters green.
He led the troops on D-Day,
In the biggest battle ever seen.

Miss Mamie likes to help folks,
And do whatever she can.
She's a popular First Lady,
With fans all over the land.

When Miss Sadie wears one of Miss Mamie's hats,
Her husband Ike teases her so,
"There goes Mrs. Eisenhower sitting in the pew.
She mustn't have anything better to do!
There goes Mrs. Eisenhower in a million dollar hat.
She looks fine. Now fancy that!"

Ike adores Sadie but he's full of fun.
She tries to catch him, but Miss Sadie can't run.
Ike Eubanks knows how to get out of her way,
And save some laughs for another day

I wonder if Miss Mamie has such fun with her Ike?
Probably not - he doesn't look like the type.

Pound The Preacher

Get some tomatoes, and a few ears of corn.
Raid the henhouse and get some eggs.
Apples, peaches and a lemon or two,
Whatever you've got in your house will do.

Watermelon, cantaloupe, cabbage, potato,
Grab it up quick! We'll sort it out later.
Get a jar of jam and a slab of ham.
Put that preacher in a pickle.

Throw it all together in a great big box.
If you got 'em grab a pair of socks.

Butterbeans, pintos, black eyes too.
Whatever you've got in your house will do.
Get a pound of butter, a fistful of lard.
Gather what you can, it shouldn't be hard.

Bring any strong arms and loud voices you meet.
Sunday's the day, the new preacher we greet.
We want to make sure we set him up fine.
(No Sister Smith, you can leave off the wine!)

Strong arms will carry what we've gathered
through the door.
Loud voices will raise a hymn of praise.
Deacon, meet me this Sunday outside the church
door.
We'll pound that preacher to the pulpit floor!

Booger Patrol

My room is on the back of the house and I hate it when it's time for me to go to bed. I miss everything! I needed to think up something to keep from having to go to bed early.

I told Momma I was having nightmares about Crackers chasing me all around town wearing pillowcases on their heads and spitting wads of chewing tobacco as they ran. She told me to stop eating so much before I went to bed.

I can always count on Grandma Hattie to help me out of most any jam. I'm her baby and she thinks I can do no wrong. She fixes my stitches when they don't pass inspection and helps me put my knitting back on the needles after Momma pulls it out. Grandma set the zipper in the jumper I made because I'd taken it out so many times the material was getting thin. I told her I couldn't bear to get into bed at night and when she asked me why not, I stumbled and stammered. I told her there were monsters under my bed, waiting to gobble me up. *Monsters?* Grandma shouted. *Big ones*, I said. *Not just monsters, but huge, ugly Boogers!*

Grandma asked if I'd been saying my prayers and I told her I had. (Sometimes I do forget and Grandma says every night I don't pray, it makes the boogers bigger). I told her if she came into my room and prayed with me, I'd have a better chance of not being gobbled up by the boogers. (Everybody else is on the party line to God's ear, but Grandma has a direct connection). *There can't be boogers under my Baby's bed. I just won't have it,* my Grandma said, stomping her foot. *We'll have to work hard, but we can do it together.*

The next day, I met Grandma at the bus stop after work. She'd come through town and stopped at Woolworth's. She had some candy for me, and the biggest broom I'd ever seen! Grandma is short and she looked funny coming down the road with the broom handle over her head. She told me it was our *Booger Broom* and the second most important weapon in our fight to wrestle the boogers to a dog fall. The first weapon was a surprise and I'd find out what it was at bedtime.

For the first time since Christmas Eve, I could hardly wait for it to get dark! Grandma came in with the big broom and said she was on *Booger*

Patrol. I hopped into bed, knowing nothing could bother me with Grandma standing guard. I wanted to know what our weapon was. Grandma said she'd prayed about the situation and an angel told her boogers hate singing! They break out in big, oozing blisters and die from the itch. I could barely stay in bed because I knew boogers would be dying for sure. Grandma has the most beautiful voice in the world and we were going to sing together.

She bent down and stuck the *Booger Broom* under my bed. As she waved the broom around, she sang this *Booger Busting Song* and I was to sing too.

There's no hiding place down here.
There's no hiding place down here
Oh, I went to the rock to hide my face,
The rock cried out, "No hiding place!"
No hiding place down here.
Oh, the rock cried, "I'm burning too!"
Oh the rock cried, "I'm burning too!"
Oh the rock cried out, "I'm burning too!
I want to go to heaven as well as you!"
There's no hiding place down here.
Oh, the sinner man he gambled and fell.

Oh the sinner man he gambled, and fell.

Oh the sinner man, he gambled, gambled and fell,

He wanted to go to heaven, but he had to go

to ... Well!

There's no hiding place down here!

Whatever dust, dirt, goblins or boogers that were under my bed, got swept out of their hiding place. Grandma comes in at least three times a week to give the boogers a scare. I love having her spend time with me before I go to sleep, and she doesn't mind at all. She tells Granddad to be quiet when he says I may have her fooled, but the honest to goodness boogers recognize me as being kin to them.

Sometimes I think he may be right.

No!
(Papa Guvnor's Confession)

No to Jell-O!
It shakes more than me.
I won't eat nuthin' if through it I see.

No to Jell-O!
It makes me fart
If you like it, eat my part.

Sweet Iced Tea For Two

Terrific Tuna Salad, macaroni in the pan.
Carrot salad, cheese crackers, beets in the can.
Miss Josie only eats these things.
Sometimes she adds a few more.
She calls and gets the delivery boy to bring them
from the store.

Grandma Hattie and Miss Josie have been friends
for years.
Grandma knows how to handle all Miss Josie's
fears.
She keeps the shades all drawn and tight,
Only lets in the clerks from J.B. White's.

They bring many dresses all in size six.
Miss Josie would be in a terrible fix.
If Grandma decided to stay at home,
Josie's waist length hair she could not comb.

With pins from a powder box, Grandma fashions a
bun.
Josie's primping is never done.

Grandma arrives at 8:45 and gets Josie into the tub.
By 10:30 a.m. Miss Josie's still in, washing between
each toe.
By 11 o'clock it would be a shock if she's close to
being ready to go.

Another ten minutes she's got one leg in her
drawers.
By this time Grandma has more than just cause,
To scream and shout till the neighbors come out.
Or get her purse and come home.

She would not stray from Miss Josie's side.
For Grandma Hattie, it's a matter of pride.
By 11:45, Josie needs a heart pill.
On the vanity stool does she sit.

She inspects her face by the light of a lamp.
Everyday she has the same fit.
When she finds a new wrinkle, mole or bump,
She goes into a horrible slump.

Miss Josie puts white powder all over her face,
As white as falling snow.
She paints her lips red and blushes her cheeks,
With a pasty kind of glow.

Once she was pretty and had suitors galore.
Her brothers all doctors by trade.
But Josie married a railroad man.
Her fortunes she unmade.
Her husband provided the best he could for Josie
and her one son.

Everyday the two ladies do the same things over.
To them it must be fun.
They're very aware and take great care to keep
Miss Josie out of the sun.

Grandma brings out the jewelry case,
So Miss Josie can play with her rings.
Should she wear pearls or a broach at her neck?
These are most important things.

After all the dressing and primping and fuss,
Miss Josie is not able.
The big trip she is about to take
Is a ride to the dining room table!

She won't go out the door of her Forrest Hills
place.
Being seen for her would be a disgrace.
Her feet haven't touched the ground in so long,
None of her parts are very strong.

Miss Josie and Grandma get along fine,
They sit at the table together.
I'm not so sure what they talk about,
But it certainly isn't the weather.

Miss Josie doesn't go to anybodies' church.
(That usually gives Grandma a start).
She says she's sure Josie talks to God,
And is a good woman in her heart.

I saw her once when I went to the door.
It was time for Grandma to leave.
She patted my head and put change in my hand,
Fifty cents, I believe.

Grandma and Miss Josie do the same things,
Every day at about the same time.
I'm happy they both enjoy themselves.
It's certainly not a crime.

Grandma says heaven has no "whites only" signs.
She and Miss Josie have great designs,
Of sitting with the angels drinking sweet iced tea.
Sounds like a lovely plan to me!

Terrific Tuna Salad

2 cans of tuna (drained)

3/4 cup saltines (ground or rolled as finely as possible)

2 eggs (boiled and chopped)

1 cup sweet pickle relish

(You can use dill if you like the taste better)

1 Tbs. Mustard

3/4 cup Mayonnaise

1 tsp. Curry powder

1/4 tsp. Salt

1/2 tsp. Black pepper

Put drained tuna in a bowl and mix well with crushed saltines. Add the other ingredients and use a spoon not your hands. There'll be more tuna left in the bowl.

Huffin' and Puffin'

On Sunday mornings, we're always in a rush. No matter what we do, getting to church on time is a problem.

Greater Young Zion Missionary Baptist Church is on Forsythe Street in the old section of Augusta, and it doesn't take as long to go there as it does to get to one of Granddad's churches in the woods. He has to get there before anyone else, to light the fire in the winter, put out the paper fans from the funeral home in the summer, and put the collection plates where the deacons can find them no matter what season it is.

Granddad has been cutting grass, washing windows and doing heavy cleaning for the same three or four white families for years. (He doesn't do any of those jobs at our house, but I hear he does good work). Granddad usually buys his cars from the people he works for. Their old car becomes his new one, and by the time he gets them, they have two things for sure; plenty of miles and a mind of their own. Leaving early makes sense because we never know exactly how far Granddad's car will take us.

We iron our clothes on Saturday night, but Sunday mornings we still rush to get dressed. Grandma thinks it's a sin to show up in a church with nappy hair. Some people don't get their hair combed all the way down their neck and little knots that look tiny black seeds sprout like weeds in the part we call the *kitchen.* Momma is quick to point them out when we sit behind somebody who might be wearing the most stylish hat. *They missed the kitchen,* she'd whisper and I'd feel a pinch down my own neck. We tried doing my hair at night, but when I got up the next morning, Grandma told me I looked like I'd wrestled the devil himself to a dog fall!

I've got more than enough hair for one person and it causes lots of problems. It's the main reason none of us go to the beauty parlor anymore. One time we went to Mrs. Luvenia Pearson's School of Beauty on Twelfth Street. Mrs. Pearson knows more about hair than anyone in the world, so Grandma, Momma and I went there to get our hair fixed for Easter. Mrs. Pearson came to Augusta from Savannah, Georgia to become the very best beautician in the world. The only problem was that she was only thirteen years old and had no formal training. She had a brother and sister to take care of and plenty of determination. Luvenia Pearson could lay in Marcel waves that called out her name better than any sign posts! It was that very talent that got her into trouble.

The state inspector for beauty salons was staying at the Richmond Hotel downtown. He couldn't help but notice the smoothly laid waves and perfectly turned crown on the head of one of the maids at the hotel. He asked the lady where she got her hair done, and the maid proudly told him about the new girl who had started her own shop. Luvenia Pearson had opened a salon and was turning out hairdos that left people speechless! Her customers didn't mind that she didn't have a license, but the state inspector did. Thanks to the maid, who thought she was being helpful, the man found Luvenia's shop and promptly closed it down. He was understanding and allowed her to work with someone else until she could get a proper license. Mrs. Pearson opened a salon and decided she would turn it into a school and train others who wanted to be beauticians.

On the day we went to the school, one of the students washed my hair and put me under the dryer. When she came back, my thick mane wasn't dry, so she set the dryer again and disappeared. Momma and Grandma were at other stations in the shop and didn't notice what was going on. I think the student working on me was having a smoke and I felt like my hair was about to do the same. Sweat ran down my face and I felt hot and sick, but I didn't know how to turn the dryer off. (Before we'd left the house, Momma warned me to be still, so I didn't dare move). No one realized what was going on until I let out a loud yell and started to cry. Mrs. Pearson herself stopped what she was doing and came and got me. She gave me some candy and began to press my hair very quickly. All the while, she was talking softly in my ear, telling me what a big pretty girl I was and what pretty hair I had. She told Momma she was very sorry and didn't charge any of us for our hairdos. We haven't been back to Mrs. Pearson's and Granddad said nobody should have blamed the student who left me under the dryer. He says there was no way the poor girl could have known my hair has more rising power than a five pound bag of Martha White's Self Rising Flour!

Sunday mornings, Momma heats up the hot comb on the gas stove and tries to tame my mane, while Grandma makes biscuits and gets things in order for the chicken frying. No matter how big the rush, we wouldn't dare leave the house without fried chicken, grits and biscuits with fatback and grape jelly.

My Granddaddy can eat a whole pan of Grandma's buttermilk biscuits. It's hard to believe so little stuff can be put in a bowl and come out to be the best biscuits anyone ever tasted! They're even better after they sit a while with the jelly and the fat back in them. The jelly oozes through the biscuit, softens up the fatback and gives the whole thing a sweet, salty taste angels would leave heaven for.

Granddad used to have a fit if there weren't biscuits on the table every morning. Then he fell out of the Vaiden's second story window and landed on the pavement. The bone was sticking out of his leg and Mr. Vaiden got his friend Dr. Carswell to fix Granddad's leg almost like new. The doctor had come up with a new way of pinning broken bones back together without using a cast. Granddad joked that he was pinned at the hip! Almost everyone had a fit when they found out Granddad had broken his leg and wasn't going to have a cast. *You'll never walk again, Preacher*! The members prayed and prayed, calling each other on the telephone. When they weren't praying, they were gossiping about how Granddad was letting Dr. Carswell use him for a guinea pig. For the first time in his life, Granddad had to stay in the hospital. His leg healed just fine and he only has a slight limp, but he stopped making a fuss about having biscuits every day. Now he's all right eating a half loaf of white bread every day and having biscuits on Sundays. Grandma Hattie reasoned that the biscuits in the hospital were so bad, it ruined Granddad's taste for them. She took a bite out of one and said it was tougher than wet shoe leather and she was lucky to have come away with all her teeth.

After Momma finishes my hair on Sunday mornings, it's my job to put flour in a brown lunch bag to coat the chicken for frying. Grandma drops two pieces at a time into the bag and I shake it up and down. I like to open the bag and see the meat all white with flour. If I see any bare spots, I shake it up some more. I know the better the coating; the crisper the skin will be on the chicken when it's fried. We fry up a big platter of drumsticks, wings and backs. Those are the only parts that make the cut at our house. The fat back gets fried in deep fat after it's been boiled for a minute or two and then patted dry. It turns white in the grease and you have to hurry and take it out before it starts to turn brown. When it's just right, the skin is crispy and the fat crumbly.

When everything is done, we sit down for a quick blessing and what Granddad calls, *tank filling*. After our tanks are on full, we clear away the dishes. If we're headed to the country, I put jelly and fatback in the leftover biscuits and Momma wraps them in waxed paper. They go into a brown bag and into Grandma's purse to be eaten after the morning service is over.

Then the fun really begins with all of us dashing around getting dressed. Momma, Grandma and I all end up in the bathroom at the same time. Grandma lays everything out for Granddad, or he's totally lost. She even puts his tiepin and cuff links on the dresser. If he doesn't see some part of his outfit right away, he calls out, *Miss Hattie, what did you do with all the socks?* My Grandma always gives the same reply, *I don't know where all the socks are, but there's a pair for you on your dresser. If you'd admit your age and put on your glasses, you might be able to find your clothes before next meeting day!*

Momma and Grandma squeeze into girdles and pull up stockings. Grandma worries about crooked seams down the back of her hose. Momma wears seamless stockings because she's always in a hurry and says her seams end up looking like the twisted stripes on a barber pole. I get to fasten their stockings to their girdles in the back. I hate the flat metal supporters that are attached to the elastic that hangs from their girdles. We have a jar on the back of the toilet with extra supporters in it. Sometimes if the metal doesn't go all the way around the rubber disk, the supporter pops loose, and if you had only one fastened, the stocking drops right down around your leg. (This usually happens when you're on the way to the collection table at the front of the church when everybody has their eyes on you). You can count yourself lucky if the elastic from your girdle doesn't fly up and pop you in the rear when the supporter comes undone.

Once while riding with Granddad, I heard the sound of elastic popping when I was sandwiched in the back seat. By the time I heard the whizzing noise, it was too late and the metal supporter popped up against the side of my head! There was no way, with so much weight in the back seat that anyone was able to bend over to try and find the supporter that hit me. I will never understand how anyone can expect a tiny piece of rubber and metal to hold silk stockings up over twice the thigh, and double the leg. Momma says if David hadn't had a sling shot with him, he could have taken on Goliath anyway. All he had to do was pull on the back girdle elastic of any one of the sisters in the crowd. The metal supporter would have flown through the air, hit the giant in the center of the head and laid him out, better than any rock!

Granddad gets the prize for getting dressed first. He has less to worry about and all the work of getting his clothes ready has been done. He goes to the end of the hall and starts what Grandma Hattie calls, *huffin' and puffin'*. He takes in a deep breath very loudly and holds it for a short time, then blows it out so he knows we can hear it all over the house. If that doesn't work, he starts jingling the car keys like the bells on Santa Claus' sleigh. When the noise gets too loud, Grandma says, *Rev.Douse,* (My Grandma almost never calls Granddad by his first name) *you can go to the car. We'll be right out.* By the time he checks the tires, water and oil and plunders around in the trunk, we're out on the porch, ready to lock the front door and begin our adventure.

Grandma Hattie's Buttermilk Biscuits

2 cups all-purpose flour

1 1/2 tsp.. Baking Powder

1/2 tsp. Salt

1 pinch Baking Soda

1 tbsp. Granulated sugar

2 tbsp. Butter

3/4 Cup buttermilk

*1/3 cup lard (melted but not too hot. You don't want to kill the rise in the baking powder).

Sift the flour in a bowl with the baking powder and salt. Add the sugar. Cut in the butter. Make a hole in the center and add the buttermilk. Add the melted lard in the same hole. Add the pinch of baking soda to the buttermilk. (Don't spend too much time playing around in the dough or else the biscuits will be tough). Fold over the flour and keep turning just enough to make the dough stick together. Roll out gently on a piece of waxed paper dusted with flour and quickly use a biscuit cutter or the rim of a glass to press out biscuits. (Just press the cutter down quickly, don't twist). Put biscuits in a pan with the edges touching.

Leave them to rest for a few minutes before baking at 450 degrees for about 15 minutes.

*You can use other shortening than lard, but the biscuits won't be as light.

Fried Chicken

Some folks swear by soaking and dipping chicken in different stuff before they fry it. That's OK, but all you really need for good fried chicken is some flour, salt, pepper and good oil for frying. (Save the bacon grease to flavor the vegetables and get a bottle of Wesson oil).

Cut up one chicken. Fryers are best because roosters are tough and baking hens even tougher. Sprinkle on salt and pepper, put some white flour in a bag and drop in a few pieces at a time. Shake them around so they get coated really well. Have the oil heated in the pan. (As far as I'm concerned, you can't fry good chicken without using a big cast iron skillet). The oil is ready when it kind of makes small waves in the skillet. Don't let it start to smoke. Gently lay in the pieces and fry golden on each side. I can't tell you how long it takes. You'll just have look at the chicken and judge for yourself. Drain on paper towels. This chicken eats good cold if you're lucky enough to have any left.

Angels Watching Over Us

I believe potholes and bumps in the road call to my Granddad. He loves to hear the musical squeak of the back springs as he shakes his passengers up and down. Grandma says when she has to take medicine there's no need to shake the bottle first. She can just take a good healthy swig and immediately go riding with Granddad. To make matters worse, he's too vain to wear the glasses that were prescribed for him. I don't think he likes the way he looks with them on. Momma thinks he just doesn't want people to know he's getting old and can't see as good as he used to.

Riding with Granddad is more exciting than the rides at the Exchange Club Fair! Every year we go to the fair grounds downtown and take our chances on the different rides. We love to bounce, shake, rattle and roll and then stuff ourselves with hotdogs and cotton candy. When we ride with Granddad, it's the same thing, only after church we get to eat home cooking.

His cars look like they couldn't make it to the corner and sometimes they don't. He manages to drive all over the road and we bump and bounce like clothes in a washing machine! We kids love it, but when the ride gets too bad, Momma is the first to speak up. I guess she remembers when she was a teen and Granddad hit a big bump in the road. The door on Momma's side of the car flew open, and she rolled down a freshly graveled road. It took weeks for her to heal and needless to say, it took months before she would even consider getting in the car with her dad. My Granddad seems to have a talent for throwing people out of moving cars.

One Sunday, Granddad had two of his church members in the back seat. It was very cold and everyone was sitting close, trying to keep warm. My Grandma was up front and Granddad went around a curve. Fortunately for Grandma, he wasn't going too fast. The door popped open on Grandma's side and Granddad quickly grabbed a fistful of the tail of her coat! He was able to steer the car and keep holding his precious Miss Hattie until he could stop. There's always some rope in the trunk of the car, along with water for the radiator, tools and patches for the *maypop* tires. (they may pop at any time). After a prayer of thanks,

Granddad tied the rope on the inside of the door handle and Grandma held onto it until they got to the church. During the meeting, one of the ladies that had been in the back seat went up, sat on the mourner's bench and told the whole church she'd found religion. (She probably figured if she was going to be riding with my Granddad, she'd need a bit more insurance than Pilgrim Health and Life could offer).

My Granddad isn't the only preacher who gives his family reasons to have the shakes when they are on the road. Rev. Feltz Hart is the minister at Mount Calvary Baptist Church, across from the United House of Prayer for All People where my Grandma Essie Bell goes to church. Mrs. Hart told Grandma about the time they were driving in the pouring rain. Reverend Hart had heard if you put tobacco spit on the windshield, the raindrops ran off more quickly and you could see the road better. During a heavy downpour, he broke out a plug of tobacco he'd been saving for just such an occasion. He bit off a piece, chewed it some and went to spit on the windshield. Rev. Hart wasn't used to chewing or spitting and got the two kind of mixed up. He managed to swallow the big wad of tobacco juice he was aiming at the windshield! The poor man spent the rest of the trip lying down in the back seat trying to stop his head from spinning round and round! Mrs. Hart drove them all home safely.

Old as Granddad's cars are, they're always big. He likes to pack in members like sardines in a can. Most of the time, he has a car full of ladies and kids. He has a regular route he travels like the Pied Piper. The adults pile in first and the kids fill in the spaces. I'm happy when Granddad does have some men in the car, because they take up less room. We kids sit one up and one back like keys on a piano. Sometimes Granddad has children pressed up against the dashboard and sitting in people's laps. I've been smushed between two members with rear ends that really needed the whole seat to themselves and possibly a little extra.

I think it's funny how flesh seems to expand during a car ride. Hips start out one size at the beginning of a trip, and by the time you get where you're going, the same hips have almost doubled in size, and I think I know why this happens. When Granddad blows the car horn, the ladies have just finished dressing. They're molded into their Sears and Roebuck Catalog girdles and long-line brassieres they wear only on Sundays. I believe their skin is numb. After just a few minutes, the feeling begins to return and all that flesh, held in by so much rubber and elastic, starts to scream out to be free. Legs and knees swell up from poor circulation caused by shoes many sizes too small. The same ladies who walk in a regular way every day have their poor toes mashed together and stuffed into shoes that are way too short and tight. They have to tip along on the balls of their feet. The high heels of the shoes sink down into the soft country dirt and make walking a nightmare! Most of Granddad's members would have knocked Cinderella out and married the Prince themselves because when he'd come around looking for the foot that fit the glass slipper, those sisters had plenty practice. They would've squeezed their foot into that slipper or died trying, (especially if it looked good and had a matching purse).

I've dreamed I was in the back seat when everyone's girdle gave way at the same time. All the shoes exploded off feet swollen like puffed marshmallows. In that particular dream, I die from suffocation. Some of the other people in the car drown in a sea of oil as the hair grease and pressing wax turns liquid and all the curls and waves drop at once. My last breath is cut short by the smell of *Hoyt's Cologne* and *Evening In Paris* perfume. I think about that dream when I'm about to get into Granddad's car.

Riding with Granddad is really scary at night! We had a flat tire way out in the boonies once, and we all got out of the car. Granddad got a big flashlight; tire patches and the tire pump out of the trunk. I just knew the whole Ku Klux Klan was waiting in the bushes to snatch me away from my family while Granddad worked on the tire. Grandma told me to think about my guardian angel watching over me. I tried that, but I was still scared and every time a car came by, I knew it was *crackers* who meant us harm. When a pick-up truck came by, I jumped into my Momma's arms!

Momma tells me, *'Po Crackers are God's curse on Cain for killing his brother Abel.* That's what happened in the Bible story we read in Sunday school. Of course some white people say the curse

God put on Cain was making him dark-skinned. My Momma explained that being colored is not a problem because you can still be clean and when you fix up, no one can tell if you have money or not. Not so with Crackers! Momma says they're permanently marked with chewing tobacco stains around their mouths that won't come off, even with soap and bleach. Their stringy hair would fall out before it would hold a curl. Grandma showed me how they have to backcomb their hair to get it into some kind of style. They call it teasing and I've seen some white ladies with hair that was still laughing! I've heard lice wouldn't even take up residence in the rat's nests some Crackers call hair and they smell like dogs when they get wet.

Granddad tells people some white folks hate the trash of their race more than they dislike Jews and colored people. I think that's the reason the Crackers get so upset and call us nasty names. They say colored people ought to know their place and not try to be *uppity.* I'm not sure where my place is, but I know it's not anywhere near where Crackers hang around. I guess I'd be upset, too. Looking like they look and being an outcast from one's own people has to be tough. Momma and Grandma Hattie feel sorry for them for sure. Momma always says the Crackers are, *Too 'po to give God a good prayer.*

One time we were on Broad Street waiting for Granddad to pick us up. Grandma was looking neat and proper as always, wearing her gloves and carrying a parasol. (My Grandma does not like rays of the sunshine on her skin too long. She says her brown covering is already nicely done and doesn't need to cook any longer.) Just as we started to cross the street, some Crackers came by in a raggedy-looking truck. They were in a heap, hollering and shaking their fists at us. *Niggah! Niggah! Niggah!* My Grandma didn't even try to move any faster. She just shook her head and said, *Mercy me! There they go. Been white all their lives and ain't got nothing to show for it.* She pulled up her back as straight as an arrow, pointed her parasol high in the air and brushed off that noisy mob like lint off a new suit. We got in the car, and she started telling Granddad about one of his church members we'd seen on Broad Street. She never even gave the Crackers so much as a mention.

I told Granddad about being scared of the Klan and he said he was glad he had the good sense to sleep on his sheets. He thought his pillowcase belonged on his pillow, not over his head with eyeholes cut in it. I get the feeling my family feels sorry for the Crackers because they don't know any better and wouldn't get any prizes for being too smart.

Grandma threw away an old white pillowcase and I decided to see what it would be like to have one over my head. I got some of Momma's dressmaker's chalk and put the pillowcase over my head to mark the eyeholes. I marked them quickly because it was getting hard to breathe. I took the thing off, cut the eyeholes and put it back on. I looked in the mirror and decided the whole thing was downright creepy looking. I hadn't cut a hole for my mouth, so when I did breathe, my glasses fogged up. I looked sort of like a garden scarecrow. I think the only good thing about wearing something like that is you could get into all kinds of trouble and nobody would know who you were.

With a name like Ku Klux Klan it makes sense to me there would have to be something weird going on. I like lizards well enough but not so much I'd want to be in a club with a Grand Lizard for a leader. Grandma Hattie hates lizards and when she sees one, she usually throws something at it. Whatever is at hand goes sailing through the air and she always says the same thing, *I don't care if you do catch flies. Do it somewhere else!* I've watched the little green lizards in the yard, hop on things and change colors. I've seen white people get red in the face and I know they turn blue when they don't get enough air. I thought maybe the Grand Lizard could change his color really fast, like a neat magic trick. I asked Momma about it, and she told me the Klan leader wasn't called a Lizard, but a Wizard.

Now I'm really confused. The members of the Klan are so happy about the cross they light one on fire at every meeting, so Granddad says. (They only allow purely white folks at the meeting, so it's hard to know exactly what goes on. I guess they can tell if you chew the right tobacco, have all your stains in the right place and smell disgusting after a good rain). In between meetings they light crosses in people's yards and all over the place. I wonder why they need a Wizard around? I guess he does magic tricks by the light of the burning crosses. I tried on the pillowcase just to see how it would feel, but I'm scared of fire, so I won't be lighting up any crosses. My Auntie Geneva is always telling people who complain too much to, *Get off the cross, honey, 'cause somebody else can use the wood.* I suppose the *somebody else* Auntie is talking about must be the Klan members.

I'm pretty scared of being out at night with crazy Crackers driving around. Sometimes I get a little car sick bumping over the roads, smushed up between heavy hipped members with Granddad driving, but the food at the churches we go to is worth all of that and then some.

During the services when everyone is singing, and shouting Amen, my mind is on what I'm going to put on my plate when I get outside. Everybody's wearing their best clothes, and would say *Amen* to anything Granddad or any other preacher had to say. Things begin quietly and then quickly get out of hand with ushers in white uniforms scrambling around to attend to those who've given themselves to Jesus, or as Momma says, *Are waiting to be comforted by certain male ushers.* I do like to hear the sound of paper fans popping in the same rhythm as feet keeping time on wooden floorboards. The singing is the only part I like. I adore the end of the service and *Striking the parting hand of fellowship.* Everybody sings while holding hands, waving them up and down to the music. There's no piano being played, just the sound of the voices. At each different song verse, people turn in a new direction to hold hands with another member. By this time, I can almost taste the ham, macaroni and cheese (or macaroni pie), and the chocolate and pound cakes.

White people call the dinners after church services Potluck. At first I thought they were saying pot liquor and I couldn't understand why somebody would want to bring the juice off a pot of greens or peas to a church dinner. I don't like that name anyway, because the only luck involved is that I'm lucky enough to be present for the eating! The ladies put out the best dishes they know how to cook. Everyone is asked to bring a basket, (but it ends up being a cardboard box for most folks).

The deacons see to the hog being barbecued and pulled pork and hash are the order of the day. Most of the chicken is fried and comes from different people's baskets, but some churches put some on the same pit with the hog. I like the hash and rice, but it doesn't agree with me when we have long rides. Grandma tells the ladies to give me plain rice, which is one of my favorites. They always try to cover it with a big scoop of hash and once I even pulled my plate out of the line of fire. I'd gotten everything piled up just like I wanted it with all my favorites and a lady was about to plant a huge serving of watery-looking hash on top of all of it. I pulled my plate away, just as the hash landed on the table with an ugly sounding *splat!* Grandma was behind me in the line and explained they couldn't stay in the car with me if I ate hash. (I don't think it's fair kids have put up with adults with gas and everything else, but if something doesn't sit right on our stomachs, we don't get to eat it until we're nearly grown). Grandma helped clean up the mess and my plate was saved. My dignity was probably in question, but I had chocolate cake and that made it all right.

Every church we visit serves the food a little differently. Some have the deacons put huge pieces of plywood on big wooden sawhorses covered with plywood and spread with tablecloths so everyone can get in a line and share the food. There's usually a special table for the preachers with even more good stuff on it. There're always tables to sit down and eat, but at some churches members park their cars on the yard and serve from the trunks. People kind of ramble around, getting the dishes certain folks are famous for. Most people save the best food for friends and the visitors get the chicken necks and backs. At one of Granddad's churches in Columbia County, the ladies put red food coloring and chopped bell peppers in the potato salad. It tastes pretty good but looks like it belongs on the dinner table at Christmas.

Most people don't eat on the grounds. The fun of church anniversary food is piling it up to take home. Everything mashes together to make a flavor you can't get anywhere else. There's nothing in the world like pound cake with a smidgen of chocolate icing on it, or coconut pie with some sweet potato pie on top of it. Nobody wants to miss anything and paper plates will only pile so high. If you separate the meat and vegetables from the desserts, you have to put up with a bit of pot liquor from the greens. Sometimes I manage to get the vegetables on top of the rice and that holds the juices nicely. The trick is to get the paper napkins peeled away from the food once they soak up the grease. It's best to put the pie down first with the cake on top. No matter how you fix up your plate, whenever you eat food from church, it tastes like some more.

My Momma and her Daddy don't agree about anything. They fuss about the right way to fix the pump we use for water, and who pays for repairs. Grandma and I entertain ourselves outside while Momma and Granddad disagree inside the house.

I told Momma one of the girls from my Brownie troop at Bethlehem Community Center saw Granddad's car in her neighborhood. She saw the car on her way to school and it was still there when she got home. My friend thought Granddad might have picked me up from school, so she knocked and asked if I could come out and play. When the lady opened the door, my friend saw Granddad, napping on the sofa in his under shorts. When I told Momma, she turned a funny shade of gray. The fireworks began when Granddad got home that evening. Grandma quickly got our egg baskets and we adjourned our meeting to the hen house. I'm sure the workers at Avery Meat Packing Company on the other side of the creek, could hear Momma yelling. Even the hens were in a bad mood and kept pecking my hand when I'd reach in the nests. (If I'd known that piece of news was going to cause such a ruckus, I would've kept it to myself). Nobody talked at the supper table and everybody went to bed early with wind in their jaws.

No matter how much fussing goes on during the week, we manage to look good on Sundays and live to tell about Granddad's terrible driving. I'm happy when the car pulls into our driveway, especially at night. Momma gets out complaining she'll never go with Granddad again and Grandma starts a sermon about how nice it looks when we're all together. (She always likes for things to look nice. That's why I didn't tell her what I did with that old pillowcase).

Grandma is convinced angels are watching over us. I hope the angel in charge of looking out for my Granddad has tight lips, nerves of steel like Superman and a driver's license, just in case.

Kin Sing

Grandma sings high as angels fly.
Cousin Ham sings low as can go.
Granddaddy sings in the middle and Momma and I
fit in.
There's nothing I like better, than singing with my
kin.

You can play baseball, horseshoes or cards.
You can jump rope or ride on your bike.
Give me a piano, some cousins and a song.
There's no way I could ever go wrong.

Singing with family puts a smile on my face.
I love when we strike up a tune.
It makes me so happy I could sing all night.
They always have to leave too soon.

I'll Fly Away

Wooten Road started out as a wagon trail. The community around it went into more modern times, but Wooten Road stayed in the past. Paved roads at either end surround the dirt road: Olive Road on one end, and Fifteenth Street on the other. One of the reasons Grandma Hattie liked this house was because she doesn't drive and I think she liked the idea she could walk to the bus stop at the end of the road.

The nice thing about living on Wooten Road is that all the neighbors are friendly. The Jacksons next door have a granddaughter that I play with a lot. Vickie is small but she isn't afraid of anything and we have a good time mixing up creations and eating stuff from our grandmothers' gardens. Vickie likes eating green fruit from the trees, but not me.

We like to visit Miss Ella. She lives like people I've read about on slave plantations. She wears long cotton dresses with heavy white slips underneath. Miss Ella chews tobacco and can hit the spit cup right in the center without looking up.

She tells us about when she was a girl and worked on a farm. She got married when she was twelve and had a baby at thirteen. Miss Ella told us she thought babies came from hollow logs and when it was time for her first baby to be born, she slipped out of the house and found an old log in the woods. When her family figured out where she was, Miss Ella was on her knees with her head all the way up in the log wondering when the baby was coming out! Vickie and I just looked at each other and giggled. (Vickie thinks babies come out of cabbage heads).

Miss Ella's husband Mr. Beard is a bit gruff-looking, but he's nice. Sometimes he lets us ride in his hay wagon. In winter, Miss Ella wraps sweet potatoes in tin foil and puts them in the fireplace ashes. Few things eat better than a syrupy sweet potato that's spent a whole day at the edge of the fireplace soaking up the heat left by the burning wood. When you peel away the foil, the skin shrivels up and looks terrible, but the meat inside looks like Momma's velvet evening dress and taste as smooth as silk going down. Miss Ella gives us one to eat, and one to take home.

Some Saturdays, Vickie's Granddad, Mr. Jackson takes us on what he calls *The Pig Run.* We get in the front seat of his old truck that has the back loaded with garbage. Near the cab are neat rows of big pickle jars and steel jugs. We stop off at the dump that's not far from Wooten Road and then the real fun begins! We visit restaurants and collect the scrap food for the pigs. Mr. Jackson knows all the cooks and owners and some of them give us treats to eat on the way home. Looking at the hog slop doesn't give you an appetite and the smell is even worse, but a jar of tea from the Red Star Lunch or sweet potato pie from the Tasty Shoppe make it all worth while. We wash out the glass tea jars and bring them back for a fill up on the next trip.

Once a year the folks on Wooten Road come together for a hog killing. Mr. Jackson hits a huge hog in the head with a bat. (He used to shoot the hog in the head, but the ladies complained about having to fish the bullet out of the hog's headcheese). The men manage to wrestle the hog into the air with a block and tackle. While it hangs letting the blood drain, the ladies get ready to make sausage. Grandma brings out the grinder and everyone finds a job. Even the smallest kids find firewood to keep the huge cast iron washpot boiling with water to keep things clean. The whole road buzzes with people working together for the delight of their stomachs. The hog meat is put inside the Jacksons' smokehouse and when it's cured, everyone who helped gets some.

Behind our house is Butler Creek. We're always battling large rats that come to the creek bank for food. The meat packing plant on Olive Road dumps stuff into the water and sometimes it has a red tint to it. The animals come to eat the scraps and find their way into the house. We have huge traps with chains but the rats are pretty smart at getting the big hunks of cheese out without springing them.

Ever since I can remember, grown folks have warned me about playing near the creek bank. The county stockade is right around the corner and when the weeds on the creek get tall, a crew of men is brought out to clean it up. From our back porch, I saw a work crew and decided to get a closer look. Grandma was busy, so I headed for the fence that separates our property from the creek. Near the edge of the water were about eight men dressed in white uniforms with blue stripes down the pant legs. Most times I'd see the work crews and go about my business, but they were singing! The swing blades waved in the air in rhythm. I ran toward the fence, to see if I knew the song. They weren't chained together like some of the gangs that work on the roads. It was blazing hot and the men were covered with so much sweat, I thought they'd taken a dip in the creek. One guy looked very young and he kept trying to keep the big drops of sweat out of his eyes. As I got closer to the fence, the crew took one step closer to the water. I was happy because I'd never been too close to any prisoners and I wasn't sure what they'd do, if anything. There was a guard with a shotgun standing like he was ready to shoot at any second. I watched and listened for a moment, but I didn't know the song they were singing. I was about to go into the house for my jackstones when I heard a splashing noise and saw the younger man I'd been watching break away from the others. He headed in the direction of the main road with escape on his mind. It felt like I was in a dream, but I heard the guard with the gun shout, *Halt!* He said it more than once and everything seemed to speed up with voices sounding like growls that I couldn't understand. The man kept moving as quickly as the muddy creek water would let him. I felt my own heart pounding with each of his steps, and for some reason, I hoped he'd get away. I heard what sounded like a firecracker pop and I saw smoke in the air just as the prisoner fell face first into the creek.

I opened my mouth to scream, but for the first time in my life, nothing came out. I ran toward the house as fast as I could, jerking and hopping like a chicken with no head. My brain was in a fog and couldn't tell my body parts how to work right. I wanted to go back and see if the man was dead, but I was too scared. My head ached and I wanted to have somebody's arms wrapped around me. Grandma must have come out of the house when she heard the noise. The tail of her dress was flapping in the wind as she moved quickly toward the fence. She was glad to see I was still in one piece, but didn't want to show it. (Grandma acts as if everything needs to be a secret). She tried to look mean and said, *I told you to stay away from that creek!* I dropped my head and bit my lip, but the tears came in a flood. I didn't know what else to do. We could hear sirens blaring and Grandma put her arms around me and headed toward the house.

We found out later that lots of people showed up on the creek bank that day, but I ended up in the house lying on the sofa. Grandma gave me a Coke-Cola and a Goody Headache Powder and we talked about whether to tell Momma what happened. We decided she'd find out anyway and I was ready to hear her holler at me for being where I had no business.

Later that evening, Granddaddy reported that the prisoner had only been wounded. Momma didn't yell at me at all, but it might be a while before I play near Butler Creek again.

Some drivers use Wooten Road as a cut-through to Olive Road where the traffic is. They turn onto the road at break-neck speed, only to discover the sharp curve about half way to the other end. Right in the center of the curve sits a big tree, like a soldier minding his post. If a driver doesn't straighten up fast, he ends up hitting the tree head on. Our house is right before the curve, and we've had our share of crushed fences when drivers looked up, saw the tree, and tried to get right before they struck disaster.

One day at the mailbox across the road, I heard a car coming. I knew from the sound of things, it was going too fast to straighten up before the curve. I've always been happy that my dog, Snoopy is too smart to chase cars. I've had Snoopy since he was a tiny fur ball. His mother, Tang, belonged to the Brooks, who live in Gilbert Manor Housing Project, where Momma works. Tang runs loose all around the project and everyone knows her. When Snoopy was born, Tang had seven other puppies and the Brooks boys were looking to give them away.

I went and saw the puppies under a house across the street from the projects. Butch, the youngest Brooks, told me he thought the little fuzz ball with brown and black spots was the one for me. He explained how adults couldn't resist puppies and if I wanted to keep the dog, I had to make sure I got Momma to hold him right off the bat. Butch even offered to go with me to the Social Room to make sure thing went my way. I knew Momma would say it was all right, but Grandma would need to be convinced. Just as we thought, Momma caved in when she saw the puppy, who I'd named Snoopy. (He's my favorite of the Peanuts Gang).

When we got home, I put him behind the kitchen door when Grandma wasn't paying attention. After supper, Snoopy began to howl as loud as he could! Grandma jumped up and threw the door back. When she glared down at Snoopy, he gave her his most pitiful, big eyed, puppy look. There was no way he was going back to the projects, and we've been pals ever since. He eats whatever I eat, loves to romp in the creek, and bark at the hogs. He's a great watchdog and knows when it's time for everyone to come home. My dog roams the neighborhood during the day, but arrives in time for supper. Granddad stops at the Chinese store for liver cheese and Johnny Cakes and he's taught Snoopy to sit up and beg for the tiny bit of fat around the meat slices. Sometimes Snoopy can look pitiful enough to convince Granddad to give him a piece of meat and a few crumbs of a Johnny Cake. I have a leash for him, but we only use it when he goes for a ride in the car. Snoopy knows everyone on Wooten Road and they know him.

I watched his ears stand straight up, as we got ready for the speeding car to try and take the curve. From the safety of the porch, we watched as the driver tried to straighten up. It looked like the tree reached out and grabbed the car, because it picked up so much speed, there was no way it was going to stop. Both Snoopy and I were glued to one spot on the porch as we watched.

At the sound of the crash, Snoopy's ears perked up even higher and it took a second before we could undo our parts from the porch. We ran down the road with Snoopy barking the whole way. I'd seen dead people in caskets at funerals, but never before the funeral home fixed them up in their best Sunday clothes. I was certain the driver had to be dead. When the car hit the tree, the horn got stuck so those people in the neighborhood, who didn't hear the crash, heard the blaring car horn. As I got closer, I could see steam coming from the hood of the car, which looked like an accordion, pressed up against the big tree.

I peeped in the window and saw that the driver was a white man and he was still alive! His head was leaned back against the seat and I saw a trickle of blood on his forehead. His hand was hanging out the window with a whiskey bottle in it and he was singing to the top of his lungs, *Some glad morning when this life is o'er, I'll Fly Away*! He couldn't sing very well and only got a word right every now and then, but it didn't matter since I guess he was celebrating being alive. (He didn't look like the type that needed much excuse for a party). For a split second, he and his car did seem to fly away.

Everybody ran out to see what was going on, and Grandma called the sheriff. The living and the dead must use the same transportation, and in minutes, a hearse arrived. The man kept singing and loading himself with liquor as the attendants loaded his skinny frame into the hearse for the trip to the hospital. The deputy said the guy was lucky to be alive. I used to like to sing *I'll Fly Away* in church, but after hearing that hillbilly, off key version, it just doesn't seem the same.

The Ride

The cars are lined up, not a seat to spare.
The mood of the people is grim.
They have a job to do. It's nothing new.
Frankly, I'll be glad when we're there.

We ride through the county, not much to be said.
This isn't the happiest time.
I can think of places I'd rather be.
At least I get to sit on my Momma's knee.

There's that dreary building, looking so lost.
"Baby you can stay in the car"
Your mind must be gone. I'm not sitting alone!
I've come much too far.

I'll hold on tight to my Momma's skirt.
Make sure she comes out of that booth.
When she pulls that curtain, I want to make certain,
When it opens, she'll still be there.

Go get your neighbor, and tell all your friends.
There's no longer a tax or a test.
Get a ride or give one. Hold hands if you must.
Momma says in God we must put our trust.

People have tried. Some have died
To do what we came for today.
We might be scared, but we're prepared.
We won't be turned away.

Diary of the Rich

Summertime is my favorite time of the year. I have my birthday on July 17th to look forward to, and there are all kinds of good things to eat blooming and blossoming. There's nothing better than sinking my teeth into a big, juicy peach and having the juice burst out and run down my neck. It's downright fun! I could eat a washtub of watermelon on any day of the week. Most people like it ice cold, but I like mine right off the truck or out of the field.

Once a week the _Vegetable Man_ comes to Wooten Road. We call him that, but he sells some of everything good to eat on his truck. He has whatever is in season. Sometimes he even has small pieces of streak-o'lean bacon to go into the collard or turnip green pot. He comes down the road blowing the truck horn as he hollers loudly, _Vegetable Man! Get your vegetables!_ We can hear his old truck squeaking way before it gets close to our door. It has a top over the back that looks like it might have come off a huge turtle. He keeps the scales hanging from the top of the shell in the back, and the three chains that hold the tin basket make a jingling noise when the truck moves. Folks come out of their houses and stand in the road behind the truck to buy whatever they want. Wherever he stops he gives samples, so folks eat and talk. Momma says the *Vegetable Man* knows the gossip from one end of town to the other. Sometimes folks buy fifty-cents worth of fruit to get two bushel baskets of who's doing what.

The watermelons on the vegetable truck are the best in the world! He always has one cut open so you can see how good they look inside. He says if you don't like the melon you get, when he comes by next time, he'll give you another one free. We've never taken him up on the offer because the melons we get are always ripe, red and sweet as sugar. Sometimes Grandma thumps the bottom with her thumb and first finger. If it makes the right sound, I get to carry it to the pump house out back. She mashes the bottom of the cantaloupes, sticks them under her nose and sniffs. The whole truck usually smells like melon to me, but Grandma always picks good ones.

When we hear the vegetable truck, Mrs. Jackson, our neighbor and her granddaughter Vickie come out too. Vickie is younger than I am and we play together a lot. She acts a little wild sometimes, but if I tell her I'm going to go back home, she settles down. Grandma and Mrs. Jackson talk while they thump and mash melons. The *Vegetable Man* gives Vickie and me some muscadines or a peach to eat while our grandmothers visit and talk. When the melons and other fruits have been picked out and money paid, Grandma goes into the house for the big kitchen knife to cut open one of the watermelons.

The pump house covers the electric well. Grandma built it with tin on top, just the right height for working on things. Momma says we get The Augusta Chronicle newspaper to read the Colored News and use the rest to put over the pump house when we clean fish, pluck chickens and do any kind of messy jobs. Grandma puts the eggs in a covered basket and people come by, get what they want and leave the money in the same basket. Sometimes we leave plums, apples or grapes on the pump house for the taking.   I don't think I've ever eaten watermelon inside the house. Vickie and I like to sit on the back porch steps and see who can spit the seeds the farthest into the backyard. Vickie is smaller than I am, but she can nearly spit all the way to the creek! We have to rake up the seeds or else they'd sprout into a melon patch in the yard. Most of the time, the chickens come around and peck them up for us.

When I eat watermelon, I just stick my face right down into the flesh. The juice gets all over me, and flies, buzz back and forth across my face. I'm sure when the flies see the vegetable truck on Wooten Road, they know somebody is about to cut open a watermelon. They seem to arrive before the knife can make the first cut through the rind. I know flies must hang around for a reason, but I haven't figured it out yet. Watermelon is just too juicy! The mess it makes gives Vickie and me a good excuse to wet ourselves down with the water hose.

Momma gets upset when she sees pictures of grinning colored kids eating watermelon. She says ignorant white folks draw them to make fun of colored people. The kids are black as shoe leather with wiry braids standing straight up all over their heads. Any child around here with a nappy head like that would have a date with a hot comb quick as a flash! Grandma told me colored people started using the hot comb because the heat killed lice. It wasn't until later people started wanting straight hair.

I wish I could draw better than I can. I'd make pictures of Cracker children eating banana and mayonnaise sandwiches. They'd have buckteeth, with ugly faces and hair. I'd sell the pictures to colored people so they could have a good laugh. Momma say it's a blessing I can only draw stick people because the world already has as much meanness as any of us can stand.

Ugly pictures or not, I still like watermelon. I eat mine with a fork because Momma won't let me hose myself down every time I eat some. Granddad eats all the melon and then drinks the juice out of the rind. Grandma gets after me when I scrape down into the rind. We cut it up to make the best pickles in the world.

In the backyard we have plum, apple, and pear trees. Vickie puts salt on the green fruit and eats it like some kind of treat. That taste puckers up my mouth and has to be punishment for pulling the fruits off the trees before it's ripe. One of my favorite places is the bench under the grape arbor. We pick grapes by the washtub full and make jelly and wine. From the arbor bench, I can watch the chickens, turkeys, and ducks strut and waddle around the yard. I can hear Mr. Jackson's pigs squeal and grunt in their pen just over the fence. Some parts of them usually end up on our table.

Grandma peels sugar cane stalks from the Jackson's garden and Vickie and I chew it and suck the juice. (Sugar cane is not for anyone that doesn't like to chew).

I believe we must be some of the richest people in the world! I hear Granddad saying we're poor, but I think he's confused. We have all the food we can eat, running water and a bathroom inside the house. We can cook, sew, do most anything with a needle and everybody can play the piano. We have a hi-fi to play and a TV to watch. If anybody is any richer, I can't imagine what all they have. As far as I'm concerned, we've got everything we need and then some.

Obie Jr's Harley

Obie Jr's got a Harley.
It's bright and shiny as can be.
With boots and leather jacket on,
He's quite a site to see.

The Harley's big and Jr's no shrimp.
Grandma calls him an overgrown imp.
But she winces if someone else complains.
"They're not family, it's just not the same".

Obie Jr's got a Harley,
He rides folks on the back.
Attention from ladies
My Cousin never lacks.

Sunday is race day.
Obie's at the track.
Nine times out of ten,
He's leading the pack.

He's a crowd favorite.

They clap and they roar.

The faster he goes,

The crowd wants more.

I'm glad he's my cousin.

I think it's divine.

I'd like to ride on his Harley sometime.

But I don't want to kill Grandma,

She'd have a duck fit,

If on Jr's Harley,

My bottom I'd sit.

I'll be content to stand on the side,

And cheer for the others who care to ride!

The Operation

It's a good thing turkeys taste good because they're pretty dumb! No matter how they move, they look ridiculous. When they run, it seems the red wattles under their necks seem to move faster than they do and their beady little eyes make them look like they're always up to no good.

Grandma likes to stand at the fence and talk to Mrs. Jackson. They can visit with each other for hours. No one in our house eats hot peppers, but Grandma has a small bush in her garden. She cans them for her brothers and anyone else who comes to visit. Some people like the juice poured over their collard greens. Grandma strings the pods together and hangs them in the kitchen, because the pretty red color says *Welcome!*

I like red. I'm not sure how the store clerks know that though. When we go shopping, the first thing they bring out is always red. If it's something we can do without, Momma always leaves the store. The color red got one turkey in big trouble.

One day as Grandma talked to Mrs. Jackson, she had a few pods of red pepper in her hand. Mrs.

Jackson said something funny, and as they laughed, the turkey walked up behind her and snatched a pod of pepper from Grandma's hand! (He didn't have to reach up far because Grandma is so short.) He gobbled up the whole thing!

The chicken yard went haywire! The turkey began to hop and jump around as his insides heated up! He took on everything in the yard. He even pecked the big rooster! Hens, ducks, guineas and geese were getting themselves out of the mad turkeys path! He looked like he was doing a rain dance, leaping up and down and shaking his feathers.

Vickie and I were outside and we tried to catch him. He dashed past both of us and we fell on the ground laughing! He's hotter than *Mingo's mush*! Grandma told us as she went for the water hose. (I didn't know who Mingo was, but I didn't want him cooking anything for me to eat). Vickie turned the water on at the pipe and it sputtered and spat. Finally Grandma aimed a blast at the turkey. He kept running, shaking water every which way. Everyone had come to the yard and was doubled over with laughter watching Grandma chase the bird with the hose. Every now and then she'd hit him with a full blast of the water, but for the most part, he was way ahead of her. Feathers were flying and the squawking and quacking was loud enough to bust an eardrum.

The turkey hopped and jerked like he'd swallowed a whole box of Mexican jumping beans! Finally, Momma got an old blanket and she and Grandma threw it over the confused bird and wrestled him the to chopping block. It was nowhere near Thanksgiving, but we enjoyed the turkey and dressing anyway.

Grandma Hattie doesn't grow hot peppers anymore. The ones in the kitchen now are made from wax.

Momma won a live turkey playing bingo at the Catholic Hall! Grandma named him *Emma's Folly* and he had to be the biggest turkey I'd ever seen.

After a few weeks we noticed the turkey was getting thinner. Momma was heartsick and told us to put him out of his misery. I didn't care so much about the bird, but I didn't want to have to eat anymore turkey. I was happy with Grandma said she had another idea for *Emma's Folly*.

It was summertime so the next morning when Momma went to work, I stayed home with Grandma. I knew she had something up her sleeves besides her arms. As soon as Momma was gone, Grandma told me to catch the ailing turkey. It wasn't difficult since the silly bird was starving to death. Grandma tied his feet and we noticed he had a peach pit stuck in his neck.

Grandma covered the pump house with newspaper with an old white sheet on top. We boiled water and cleaned our tools for surgery. Cousin Ellen, Grandma's niece, graduated from the Lamar School of Nursing. Miss Lucy Laney began the school so colored girls would have the chance to become nurses. (I think my Cousin Ellen looks so important in her white uniform. I really like her blue cape lined with red). Grandma tied an old meat apron around my waist so I wouldn't get turkey blood on my shorts. I felt like a nurse helping my Grandma, the doctor.

Grandma held a cloth over its beak, and the turkey's beady eyes rolled back in its head. I'm not sure what was on the cloth, but it made him seem dead. We had to get the pit out of the way so he could get food in his tummy again.

We cleaned the skinny neck with cotton soaked with alcohol. Grandma sliced open the turkey's throat with a shiny new single-edged razor blade. There wasn't much blood, but I had a sponge to get it out of the way so Grandma could see. The sun was bright, and we had a clear view of the peach pit. It had turned crossways in the turkey's thin throat and the sharp edges were hung in the skin. With the tweezers, Grandma lifted the pit out. The only nylon thread we had was black so Grandma made neat stitches in the bird's neck. We swabbed on a bit of iodine and decided the wound would heal better without gauze over it. We laid the turkey in a box on the back porch and after a few hours, it began to wake up. We put him back in the yard just before Momma came home from work.

The next day the turkey was weak-legged, but moving. We hand fed him until he got better. Momma was very happy her *Folly* was going to live and I was happy we weren't going to have to eat any more turkey until Thanksgiving.

In The Back Door

I will never understand why some white folks have to have their things separate from ours. After all, colored people do most of the cooking, cleaning and taking care of white babies. We're supposed to sit in the back of the bus and be the last to get waited on in the stores.

Granddad cleans at Mrs. Catravas' house and does the yard work. She's in charge of the Christian Science Reading Room downtown and Granddad cleans there also. She teaches piano and Granddad told her I was taking lessons from Sister Mary Ailbee at the Convent. Mrs. Catravas asked Granddad to bring me to her house so I could play for her. He asked Momma and she said it would be all right for me to visit.

When the day came, I took a bath and put lotion on my arms and legs. (Momma says nobody should ever go out looking ashy). Grandma Hattie fixed my hair just the way I like it with a ponytail and bangs. I put on my prettiest dress and looked just like I was going to church on Sunday. Just as we were ready to leave, Granddad mentioned Mrs.

Catravas told him to make sure we didn't use the front door of her house.

We were all standing in the kitchen, and for a second nobody moved. My Momma's color changed two times darker, and her whole body began to swell up. I knew from the look on Emma Washington's face, I'd be a grown woman with children of my own before I'd ever see Mrs. Catravas in the flesh!

Grandma grabbed my hand and snatched me out of the kitchen. Before I could catch a breath, my Sunday dress was up over my head and back in the closet. She handed me one of my everyday dresses and quickly marched toward the back door. I was almost running to keep up, as I tried to wiggle into the dress and kick off my Sunday shoes at the same time. Snoopy crept quickly behind me with his tail tucked. Grandma sailed across the back porch, picking up the grape baskets without ever looking down. I knew it wasn't a good time to talk and I was hoping she'd strike up a hymn.

We could hear Momma's angry voice and then the sounds of Granddad trying to start the car.

It sputtered and coughed, but finally fired up, and I ran to the driveway just as it disappeared around the curve in a cloud of dust. Grandma and I stayed outside under the arbor until Momma called us in for supper.

After we ate, I played the piano piece I was going to play for Mrs. Catravas. Momma taught me a song she'd learned for the church choir. She gets the sheet music at H.L. Greene's Store. I was glad when Granddaddy came home. We were all singing and he joined in.

Poor Mrs. Catravas just doesn't know what she missed!

Woes From Toes

My family doesn't mind working to have good eats to share and I like going to my Cousin Ellen's house for the fruitcake making. We shop for all the fixings at H.L Green's on Broad Street. We go there a lot, because it's where we change busses for the ride home after Momma gets off work. There're bushel baskets filled with peanut brittle and coconut candy at the front of the store. The green and yellow buses marked *Southeastern Stages* pull in one behind the other, filled mostly with maids wearing all kinds of different uniforms.

One evening an old lady came up to me and said. *Little girl, do you know where the Nigger toes are?* (I know where everything is in Green's, but I'd never heard of anything like that.) Momma doesn't allow me to say that word and I quickly told her, *No Ma'am.* The lady looked really tired and disappointed, and I figured if anybody could find what she was looking for, Momma would be the one. She was in the music department and as we went, the lady told me she'd been in town all day and had to get the stuff for her fruitcake. I couldn't figure out why anyone would want somebody's toes in their fruitcake, but Grandma says I ask to many questions and I didn't want to give the lady a headache.

Momma was leaving the music department and she could see there was something on my mind. The lady spoke up and said what she was looking for. I stepped back and got ready for Momma to get angry, but she smiled instead! With the lady following her, Momma headed toward the aisle where the fruitcake mixings were! The lady went up to the counter and said, *Give me one pound of Nigger toes, please Ma'am.* The young white girl behind the counter wore a hairnet pulled down almost to her eyebrows and she didn't even blink! She quickly scooped up some Brazil nuts that made a loud rattling noise as the clerk dumped them into the metal basket of the scales. As she reached for a brown bag, I hollered, *Those ain't nobodies' toes!* There were other people at the counter, and they all laughed, including Momma. *We'll talk about it later*, Momma said as she firmly gripped my hand. (That's Momma's signal for me to hush up until it's just the two of us talking).

I learned that some white person thought the
Brazil nut looked like some colored person's toe
and the name stuck. Momma said she didn't like
the name but lots of people had no problem with it
and didn't even know what the nuts were really
called. Since that ugly name had never been used in
our house, I had no idea what the lady was talking
about. When we got our fruitcake fixings I took out
a Brazil nut and held it up against my big toe. The
two were brown all right, but I didn't think they had
anything else in common.

The recipe we use for making fruitcake
came from Great-Grandma Donnie. Momma has a
copy written in a small brown paper-backed
notebook. The pages are faded, but Momma's neat,
perfectly formed printing is easy to read. Everyone
has a job to do. My cousin Sandra and I get to shell
nuts. The adults dice fruits and mix batter. The
smell of spices fills the house along with the sounds
of everyone enjoying everyone else's company.

The cooled fruitcakes are wrapped in
cheesecloth soaked in brandy. Some get the same
treatment with fruit juice. We save tins all year
round to have enough to store each cake. One large

cake gets shared right then so everyone can see how the batch turned out. Everybody *ooh's* and *aah's* when the first slice is made.

Each clan takes tins of fruitcake home to age until Christmas. The men get a sample from the first cake sliced. Grandma puts aside a small tin for Granddad who likes to sneak a piece every now and then. He carefully wraps it back up and everyone pretends they don't know he's eating it.

Get some family and some friends to help with the shelling and chopping. Make enough cakes because they'll want to share the eating too. This recipe makes about 16 pounds of cake batter. 8-10 loaves.

Great Grandma Donnie's Fruitcake

1 lb. Butter	1/2 lb. Brazil Nuts (chopped)
1 lb. Brown sugar	1 lb. Seedless raisins
12 eggs	2 tsp. Grated nutmeg
1 lb. Plain flour	1 tsp. Cloves
1 tsp. Baking powder	1/4 tsp. Baking soda
1/2 tbsp. Allspice	4 tsp. Cinnamon
4 lbs. Mixed candied fruit	
1/2 lb. Pecans	1/2 lb. Walnuts
1/2 lb. Almonds	8-10 oz. Blackberry Jam
1 lbs. Dried figs	1/2 lbs. Dried Cherries
1/2 lbs. Dried Apricots	1/2 Cup Crystallized Ginger
1 Cup Molasses	2 tsp. Salt
1 lbs. Pitted Dates	Cheesecloth
1 Bottle of Brandy (at least 3 cups)	

Combine chopped fruits and nuts (except raisins) with jam and 1cupBrandy and soak at least 2 hours (Overnight is better).

Preheat oven to 250 Degrees.

Pour boiling water over raisins and let stand for 5 minutes. (Drain)

Put raisins in a bag and dust with a bit of flour.

Sift flour with baking powder, soda and salt. Set aside.

Cream butter.

Combine sugar with butter 2-3 tablespoons at a time.

Add spices and Molasses.

Add whole eggs, one at a time.

Add flour to creamed mixture a few tablespoons at a time.

Alternate with 1 cup Brandy until all the flour is added to the creamed mixture.

Add everything together, including floured raisins.

Line cake pans with waxed paper, then grease and dust with flour.

You may use, tube pans or loaf.

Bake for 2-3 hrs. Test with a broom straw. (Make sure you wash it first).

Place pan of water under cake pans and keep it full during baking.

Cool in pans. Then on racks.

Wrap in cheesecloth soaked with brandy or fruit juice.

Store in airtight tins.

White Water

The *For Whites Only* signs over the water fountains in H.L Green's really bother me. I'd seen the signs before, but I spend more time in Green's than any other place. They have cloth in the back. It's stacked up as high as possible on tables and more comes in boxes each week. Momma loves picking through the piles and when she gets off work some evenings, we head to Broad Street. If there is a new shipment of fabric, I know how to amuse myself until Momma searches for hidden treasure among the yard goods.

I know where everything is in the store and I like walking up and down the aisles pretending I'm the boss. I pretend it's up to me to keep the merchandise looking neat. It's also up to me to count all the money at the end of the day. I pretend I have a big box of money and get someone to carry it to the bank for me. Sometimes I even look through the cloth myself with an eye for something that would look good on my Barbie doll. Grandma has been helping me make clothes for her. There are so many scraps at home; I can find plenty to keep Barbie looking good.

In the late afternoons on weekdays, there aren't many people in the stores downtown. One day Momma and I got off the bus in front of Green's. One of the clerks had told her there was going to be a new shipment of cloth coming in that morning and Momma wanted to get into it before it was all picked over. I knew she was going to be busy for a while, so I decided to walk around the store. I made my usual visit to the toy department, but I couldn't get interested in anything special. I walked up and down the aisles one after the other, but nothing looked special to me.

Then I saw the water fountains. All three of them sat there as if they were looking back at me. There was a large one with a big *White Only* sign over it. Next to it was a smaller fountain with a wooden step in front. A few feet from the shiny, new looking fountains was a broken down, sad fountain with the water running all the time. The handle on the faucet was broken and the sign above it looked just as bad. A black sign with white letters read, *Colored.* The whole thing was dingy and somebody would have to be very thirsty to take a drink from it.

I'd seen the fountains many times, but this was the first time I'd been around them when no one was watching. No clerks or shoppers were anywhere near. It was a perfect time to finally see exactly what the white folks were hiding. I would finally get to drink some water from the *White Only* fountain. My knees shook just thinking about it. I knew I was taking a big step. Would white people's water kill me? Worst of all, maybe I'd turn white and colored people wouldn't like me anymore. I had to take the chance anyway. If anyone saw me, I would just say I was thirsty and made a mistake. Most of the clerks knew my face from being in the store so much. They would just go the cloth department and get Momma. I ask questions all the time and she would probably just tell me not to try that again.

No one was paying any attention, so I quickly ran up the smaller fountain. I climbed up onto the wooden step and looked behind me to make sure I was still alone. The beige knob on the spigot was easy for me to turn. I watched the water run down into the basin of the fountain and it looked just like regular water.

My heart was pounding fast, and my hands were so sweaty I could hardly hold onto the knob. I took a deep breath and waited for my life to flash before my eyes. Momma told me just before a person dies, their whole life comes into their mind in a flash. I knew the water could kill me, but the only thing I saw in my mind was me sitting at my piano recital, trying to remember my piece, *Turkey In The Straw*. Maybe I hadn't been alive long enough and what should have been a flash was just a drop. I closed my eyes, leaned down and took a big swallow. I hopped down off the step and ran down to the end of the one of the aisles. My mouth was filled with water, but my throat wasn't working at all! Try as hard as I could, I couldn't swallow!

My cheeks were puffed out, filled with water and I figured I'd better go and get help. Momma was busy digging in a box of cloth pieces. I pulled at her skirt, and without turning around, she told me we would get a hot dog before we left the store. I couldn't talk with the water in my mouth, so I pulled at the hem of her skirt again. She thought I was playing some kind of game. I was moaning as best I could through a mouthful of water. Momma turned away from the cloth long enough to place both hands on my face, smile and squeeze in my cheeks. I gave one big gulp and felt the water go down my throat all at once. I fought the urge to spit because it would have sprayed all over Momma. I wouldn't have had to worry about the white people's water killing me because she would have finished me off, right on the spot! Momma went back to her cloth box and I went down my favorite aisle in the toy department to die, or turn white, whichever came first.

I carefully looked at my hands to see if I was changing colors. On the way to the toy department, I looked at myself in a vanity mirror on the cosmetics aisle. My eyes were still brown. I felt the same as always, just a bit scared. Finally Momma came to the toy department and said it was time to go. I was happy she still recognized me.

The lunch counter at H.L. Green's is my favorite of all places downtown. (The one in the back of course). The one up front is for white people and I hear the hotdogs aren't as good. The back counter doesn't have nice booths like the one up front. There are stools to sit on, but they aren't the most comfortable seats around. The hotdogs, fries and drinks make up for the way the whole thing looks and Momma knows we have to get a hotdog whenever we are in the store.

I was afraid to tell Momma I'd taken a drink from the white fountain because I didn't want her to worry in case I wasn't going to make it. I decided it was best not to say anything.

After we got home, every few minutes for the rest of the evening, I looked in the mirror in the bathroom to see if I'd changed at all. My heart didn't feel weak, but I wasn't sure how a dying person is supposed to feel. No one had to argue with me to go to bed that night. I lay there waiting for something to happen. I put on my very best nightgown and took my favorite pink teddy bear to bed with me. I pulled the string in his navel and listened to the music box play *Let Me Call You Sweetheart*. I thought maybe I would fall asleep and wake up the next morning white as snow. Granddad would wonder where the little white girl in my bed had come from. Grandma would fall down on her knees in prayer and I don't know what Momma would do. Maybe dying in my sleep would make things easier for everyone. I was afraid to close my eyes.

The next morning, I was happy to hear the rooster crowing! I had all my parts and I realized I was still breathing. I was so happy! I rushed into the bathroom to look at myself. I was the same color as always and everything was in the right places.

I'm more than happy to report the results of my experiment: colored people who drink from fountains with *White Only* signs don't turn white or die. The next time I go into H.L. Green's store and see the drinking fountains with the *For Whites Only* signs, I'll just giggle and say to myself, *That's what you think!*

The Maidmobile

Momma bought a car and learned to drive.
We don't have to ride the bus.
It's so much nicer. We go where we please.
Momma learned to shift gears with ease.

Our car is big! It's two shades of blue.
I like to ride in the back seat.
We ride through town with the windows down,
And pick up maids off the street.

Momma went for a license and passed both tests.
At the counter she made a request.
"I'd like my free license, I'm the widow of a vet.
My papers are signed and in order".
The man at the window stared her in the face.
"Gal, you won't get no free license in this place!"

Momma gathered her papers.
Her friend drove us home.
There she picked up the telephone.
Give me Pete Wheeler of the D.A.V.
"They won't give me my license free!

I won't pay a cent for what's rightfully mine.
Thank you Sir, that would be very kind"

The next day there was a knock at our door.
Mr. Wheeler wore a cap with a pin.
"We will straighten this out, without a doubt.
Ladies please step into my car.
It won't take long to right this wrong.
You're entitled to what you seek.
I'm here to help. It is my job,
On behalf of veterans I speak".

When we stepped through the door,
The clerk knew the score.
It was the same man she'd talked to before.

He didn't call her gal or missy or Jane,
He called Mrs. Washington by her name.
He gave her a small blue and white card.
I couldn't understand why it'd been so hard.

We left the place with the man disgraced.
I crossed my eyes and stuck out my tongue.
He wasn't aware he'd pushed the wrong pair.
(Both Momma and I are high strung).

Mr. Wheeler drove us back to our house.
When we got out he tipped his cap.
"If you have any problems, please give me a ring.
I'm only a phone call away.
You folks are members of the D.A.V.
I'm glad I could serve you today".

Our car is known as the Maidmobile.
I ride in the big back seat.
We ride over town with the windows down,
And pick up maids off the street.

Eagles' Nests

I go from one thing to another because I can't get things together fast enough before I have an idea for something else.

Grandma Hattie took me to Moses Baptist Church for a week-long revival meeting. People came from miles around to see this preacher from up North with a big booming voice. He talked about eagles and what great birds they are. He even had a real eagle's nest at the front of the church! While Grandma went up to shake his hand at the end of the service, I was looking at the nest. I've never seen a real eagle, but I liked the way the nest looked. I was determined to make one and I couldn't get it out of my mind.

Great Grandma Donnie and Papa Guvnor live out past Beech Island, South Carolina. (It's not a real island and there's no beach). I like to visit because there's so much to do. My cousins and I had finished trying to curl my Great Grandma's hair. We'd rolled it with brown paper bag twists, and my Cousin Lil had even tried the hot curlers, but Great Grandma's soft, jet-black hair just turned under a bit. Momma says her Grandmother is Indian. Great Grandma talks about her mother who had long braids she could sit on. She died when Great Grandma was very young and her father raised the family. I see Indians on TV and none of them look like Great Grandma. Her skin is lots darker than red and she doesn't have any feathers or a horse.

While we were visiting Great Grandma's house, I decided we needed wine with dinner (I'd seen that on TV at home). We found some glass milk bottles in the barn. Grandma Hattie makes wine from the grapes on our arbor, so I knew we needed some kind of berry or fruit to start with. There were lots of chinaberries and we stuffed them in the milk bottles. They didn't have any juice, so we added water and some sugar. We made caps from tin foil held on with rubber bands. After punching holes in the caps, we poured the liquid into a bucket and threw the berries away. We poured the wine back in the bottles and took it to the house for the adults to try.

Papa Guvnor told us our wine needed time to ferment. (That meant it would smell worse than it already did but people wouldn't care because it would make them drunk). He said we needed a cellar or basement to put it in, so we buried it in a hole we dug behind the barn. We figured it would be aged just right by the next family get-together.

The eagle's nest was much more fun! We got some pine straw, hay and small twigs. We made the bottom like a basket with a big dip in the middle for the mother eagle to sit. The Reverend's nest had a few feathers in it, so we chased a hen for a donation. A big piece of Spanish moss made the whole thing look great! My cousins, Ronald and Lynchee, helped carry our nest to the house.

When my Great Grandma saw us coming up to the porch, she nearly fainted! *Fatty, what are you up to now?* (She hardly ever remembers my name. With thirteen children of her own and over fifty grands and bucket loads of great-grands, I count myself lucky she remembers anything about me.) My cousins sometimes call me *Eggshell,* but that's better than *Fatty.* Somehow I look like an egg to them. Momma says people sometimes call smart people *Eggheads* and my cousins just got the mule by the wrong end.

When Great Grandma Donnie comes around, all the adults get nervous and jumpy. Everyone is afraid of her and my cousin Ronald told me why. His Momma, Auntie Annie told him all about what happened to my great uncle George.

When my George was a young man, he married a girl named Helen. One evening he came home from working in the fields and Helen didn't have supper ready. They lived down the road from their parents and Great Grandma had decided to visit. She started up the porch as George started to beat on Helen. He made the mistake of his life when he didn't stop right then. He reached out to grab his wife and his mother dropped him to the floor with one kick to his private parts!

As my cousin Ronald was telling me the story, he doubled over and fell on the ground, jumping around like a minnow on a fishing pole. Great-Grandma kept on kicking in any spot her shoe could find. George tried to roll up in the tight ball, but it didn't help. She was determined to kill the son she'd given birth to! Helen went running down the road for help, and came back with Papa Guvnor and his shotgun, Great-Grandma was still kicking

George and he would have probably been better off being shot. Neighbors gathered and stopped Great Grandma from the killing her son. Someone went for a doctor and George got out of the wife beating business.

Great Grandma smokes a pipe, and lights up right in our living room. (Everybody else has to smoke on the porch). She's so used to the pipe that once it was in her mouth and everyone was running around looking for it. I happened to look up and see the corncob stem in her mouth. I tried to get her attention, but she refused to look at me. Finally, I told Momma where the missing pipe was. Everyone had a big nervous laugh, but I think from then on she had it in for me.

Great Aunt Geneva sent me a big box all the way from Philadelphia. It was marked, *Do Not Open Until Christmas*! I marched around that box for whole month, wondering what was inside.

Christmas morning Santa had unwrapped the box. The most beautiful doll I'd ever seen was standing in front of the tree! She had short curly hair, was the same color as me, and wore a Sunday dress with lace socks and patent leather shoes. I got some other things that Christmas, but I don't remember what they were. I wanted everyone to see my doll, so I put her in the big rocking chair by the door in the living room. She looked like she was just visiting.

On a Saturday morning, Great Grandma arrived at our house for a visit. She had a basket on her arm filled with roasted peanuts, pound cake and sweet potato pone. She walked down the hall and into the living room where she saw my doll and said, *Howdy little girl!* No one said anything and Grandma repeated her greeting a bit louder. *I said Howdy, little girl!* I was watching my Great Grandmother's shoes to make sure I wasn't about to be kicked. I stepped behind Momma and said, *That's my doll you're talking to!* Great Grandma, who is pretty tall, leaned down and touched the doll. *My God from Zion! I thought that was a real child!* She took a deep breath and sat down on the sofa. I figured my doll had to special to fool Great Grandma. I still don't think she likes me and I don't ever plan to get in the way of her feet.

On a trip to Broad Street, Great Grandma bought a big block of peanut brittle from one of the baskets in front of H.L. Green's. She'd just gotten new false teeth and she took a bite of the candy and broke three of them. Grandma Hattie and I ate the rest of the brittle while Granddad and Momma took my Great Grandma to the dentist.

Great Grandma Donnie likes for her family to be together. My favorite times are the Labor Day picnics Savannah River Lock and Dam. The park is huge with tables, grills and plenty of space for parking and playing. Momma brings equipment from the playground and the men spend hours pitching horseshoes. Most of the younger guys play football and some of the older people play cards. There's something for everyone including hymn singing and just visiting with cousins who only seem to appear at funerals and picnics.

Each household brings enough food for their own group and enough to share. Of course, it's like church anniversary with everyone bringing their best dishes. There's plenty of barbecued meat, salads, hamburgers and hotdogs, chips, drinks and desserts. Even the skies cooperate and we've never been rained out!

Cousin John, Sandra's father, takes charge of making sure all of the kids who want see the water follow him. He takes inventory before we leave and makes sure he comes back with just the right number. He says he couldn't stand the commotion if anybody came up missing! He and my Uncle Jessie are always kidding each other about taking orders from Cousin Ellen and her sister, Annie Brown. We kids love her dearly, but we know just how far we can go without getting on her bad side.

The last thing eaten is the hand-churned ice cream. If you don't churn, you don't get any. It's that simple. The picnics last all day and by the time things are cleaned up, everyone is stuffed to the gills and very tired. The small paper cups of ice cream go home with everybody attempting to cram in just one more bite.

I don't have any aunts or uncles. Annie Brown is my Grandmother's niece and since all the other kids call her Auntie, she declared I would do the same. She and Momma were raised like sisters and no one in their right mind argues with Annie Brown. This is the best pie ever!

Auntie Annie's Sweet Potato Pie

4 or 5 large sweet potatoes

1 stick of butter (room temperature)

4 beaten eggs (room temperature)

2 1/2 cups of sugar

1 can evaporated milk

1 tbs. Vanilla

1 tsp. Cinnamon

1 tsp. Cloves

1/2 tsp. Freshly grated nutmeg

Boil potatoes with one tablespoon of oil until fork tender. Peel cooked potatoes and put them through a ricer. (This makes the custard smooth.)

Add butter and other ingredients. Mix well after each one.

Pour filling into unbaked pie shells. Bake at 350 degrees until firmly set in the center, about 1hr.

Makes 3 pies.

Sweet Potato Pone

3 medium sweet potatoes   1 c. milk

1 egg (Beaten)   2 tbsp. Sugar

1 c. molasses   1/2 tsp.

Cinnamon

1/3 tsp. Allspice   1/2 tsp. Salt

1/4 c. butter

Peel and grate sweet potatoes. Combine the milk, egg, sugar and allspice. Stir in molasses and salt and mix with the grated sweet potato.

Add butter on top.

Place in a cold oven and set temperature to 350 degrees.

Bake for 11/2 hours.

One of Granddad's members tasted this cake and told Grandma Hattie it was so good, *It made his tongue want to slap his brains out!*

Pound Cake

2 3/4 cups sugar

3 1/2 cups all-purpose flour

1 1/2 cups butter or margarine

6 large eggs

1/2 tsp. salt

1 cup milk

1/2 tsp. baking powder

2 1/2 tsp. Vanilla

Preheat oven to 350 degrees.

Grease and flour a 10-inch tube pan. Cream sugar and butter until light and fluffy. Blend in vanilla. Add eggs one at a time, beating well after each one. Sift flour with salt and baking powder. Gradually add to sugar mixture, along with milk.

Pour batter into pan and bake at 350 degrees for 55 to 65 minutes or until a broom straw comes out clean. Cool for 10 minutes and turn out onto rack.

Momma had Bean Pie up North and decided to give it a Southern twist! Make more than one recipe if you intend to eat any yourself.

Butterbean Pie

2 cups cooked Butterbeans (If you use canned ones, make sure they are drained)

1 stick butter (softened)

1 (14 oz.) Can Evaporated Milk

4 Eggs

1 tsp. Nutmeg

1 tsp. Cinnamon

2 tbsp. Flour

2 Cups Sugar

1 1/2 Cups Flaked Coconut

2 tbsp. Vanilla

Preheat over to 350 Degrees

In a blender mix beans, butter, milk eggs, spices and flour for 2 minutes. Add sugar, coconut and vanilla. (You won't have room for the whole thing in the blender at once, so pour some of it into a bowl and make sure you mix it together well).

Pour into pie shells. 2 deep dish, or 3 regular. (If you're taking it to church or a picnic use the regular shells.)

Bake for 1 hour at 350 Degrees.

Cool for 5 minutes on racks and wrap in plastic wrap.

Eats good hot or cold.

Colorful Ways

I love living where the weather is warm.
Folks are friendly wherever you go.
People say "Howdy" when you walk down the street.
There's no need to shovel snow.

We can be sweet and call you "Honey" or "Dear".
We don't have to know your name.
But when you visit we guarantee,
You'll never be the same.

We know how to say things in a colorful way.
"He could beg Jesus off the cross!
Steal the shortening from a biscuit
Without breaking the crust."
We know how to describe things.
Talk we must!

"He's just breath in britches.
A few bricks short of a load.
I'll beat him like white is on rice."
We can be funny, ugly or sweet.
Sometimes we can even be nice.

"He'd follow her through hell in gasoline drawers!
She first looked like one thing, then another."
Be careful, be sure who you're talking to.
It might just be your brother.

In the quiet you could hear a rat pee on cotton.
You can be rotten to the core.
Southerners can talk a wet hen dry.
Most of our food, we choose to fry.

If you're skinning a flea for his hide and tallow,
Your purse strings you might hold tight.
We paint clear pictures of what we mean.
We all do it, Colored and White.

I love living where the weather is warm.
I say "Hah Yew" when neighbors I greet.
Come sit on the porch and visit a while
Our hospitality can't be beat!

When The Saints Go Marching In

Sister Essie's in town.
Get the food basket down.
It's time for the House Of Prayer Convocation.
Essie's followed Daddy Grace to many a place.
They've been all over the nation.

Now it's time for Augusta to strut its stuff!
People look forward to the yearly parade.
All the Saints are ready to go.
The preparations have been made.

There's a whole week of meetings that heat up after
dark.
There's popcorn, candy apples and fun.
The whole of the City's on Wrightsboro Road.
Don't look for a place to park!

The church buses line Augusta's streets.
Every one of them has a marching band.
Tambourines, trombones, trumpets, and more.
All the band members know the Holy Ghost score.

Sister Essie's in town.

Get the food basket down.

Her uniform is white as can be.

She wears a pin close to her heart.

She's been with Daddy since the very start.

His picture she would never be without.

She's a faithful member without a doubt.

On Saturday night all of Augusta turns out,

To jump with the Saints and shout.

They scream and spin to let the Holy Ghost in,

They dance better than folks at a bar.

Every bell is ringing with every Saint singing,

It's the best show in town by far!

Some people laugh, some point, some giggle.

The Saints pray to be cleansed from their sins.

They're baptized once a year and they have no fear.

Sweet Daddy has what they desire.

They're happy they're whole.

Daddy helps save their souls.

They're joy is exciting and bold.

The preaching and singing goes into the night,

But the Saints have to get some rest.

The part of Convocation the people like best,

Will surely put the Saints to the test.

They must be on the good foot. Not a wrinkle or a tare.

The House of Prayer Parade is beyond compare.

Everything must be just so and just fine.

The Saints can't wait to get in line!

Every preacher in Augusta cuts his sermon time short,

In favor of the big Parade.

The members wouldn't stay. They'd pack up and go.

No one in town would miss such a show!

Colored and White line Wrightsboro Road.

The bands march in perfect step.

The crowd is delighted,

The Saints are excited!

They walk with plenty of pep.

The elders throw peanuts and candy and treats,

Blessed by Bishop Grace himself.

They scramble to the pavement and nearly come to

blows.

They don't mind stepping on each other's toes.
The big entertainment comes before Daddy's float.
Shirley Temple wows the throngs!
People clap and cheer when Shirley is near.
No better show does anyone know,
Than the one she gives her fans.

Her sparrow legs she kicks high in the air,
And twists her skinny little hips.
Under her dress she must have on
At least a half dozen lace slips.

Her real name is Beulah, but the wig she wears,
Looks just like the real Shirley Temple.
She loves the attention and the crowd loves the show.
They don't want to ever see Shirley go.

Daddy's float is the last in the line.
Everything is red, white and blue.
His fingernails are long. His voice is strong.
His hair is even longer.
He waves to the crowd, as the music plays loud.
Then they all file away for another day.

Sister Essie's in town.
Get the food basket down.

Put in some chicken and cake.

She's on to the next place with

Sweet Daddy Grace.

Have no fear you'll see her next year.

She's the one with the big tambourine.

Make sure you're ready for next year's parade

It'll be the best show you've ever seen!

Chocolate Anyone?

On a bright sunny morning the Washpot Gang noticed a strange man in the neighborhood. He had a big cotton bag swung over his shoulder and he was putting something on each doorknob. The Gang was curious and began to follow the man, keeping themselves out of sight. When the stranger crossed to the other side of the street, Emma Addie told John Lewis to grab one of the bags, so they could see what was inside.

John Lewis did as he was told and the Gang was excited to discover the pouch had candy in it! None of them could read, so the words on the box didn't mean anything. They knew it was their lucky day! Most people were at work or busy inside their houses. The Gang waited until the man left the neighborhood and collected all the bags he'd put out on Watkins Street. No one would miss what they never knew they had.

The Gang ate the chocolate candy and it didn't take much for them to get full. They hid the rest of their treasure in the bottom of an old tackle box under James Howard's porch.

They decided that catfish was on the menu for lunch, so they got a shovel from John Lewis' house and a small can for bait. As the Gang was digging, John Lewis said his tummy ached. Before Emma Addie and James Howard knew what had happened, he took off running! In minutes they were in the same race.

The adults couldn't figure out why the kids had taken up all the outhouse seats. Around nightfall, Miss Wooden ordered doses of flour water for each member of the Gang. They were weak as water, but their lips were tight as drums.

Things finally calmed down and days later, Miss Wooden went to visit a friend on a nearby street. As they talked, the lady told her that God certainly worked in mysterious ways. The woman went on to say that her husband had eaten a bit too much hoop cheese, and he needed some help getting unbound. The sample on their doorknob had been right on time! Miss Wooden whooped so loud, she nearly blew her friend off the porch! Between fits of more laughter, she explained why three little imps would never again want to see a box of Ex-Lax!

High Water

Down the rising Savannah River a goat
Did float on a great big bale of hay.
He munched on his raft and ate nearly half
Before it started to sway.

He dipped up and down while the rest of the town
Tried to keep the high water at bay.
They put coal in the rail cars to hold them on the
tracks,
But it didn't work out that way.

The hungry Savannah opened its mouth and
Swallowed everything in sight.
To the courthouse folks ran with Bibles in hand.
They'd never felt such a fright!

An angry river is an ugly sight.
A fright no one should have to see.
But the folks in the town rallied around.
Every man was put to the test.
The police paid a nickel for the Gang to reveal
any bums trying to hide and rest.

All night shovels filled bags with sand.
They sang hymns and worked side by side.
They piled up a wall and made it so tall,
The river went back in its place.
Every man on the line knew it wasn't his time
And they all sang "Amazing Grace".
The goat kept eating and the bale slowly sank.
No hymn could save it in time.
(I'm afraid to admit the same might be said
for this pitiful little rhyme).

Please don't try to eat what you use for a seat.
Don't chew on the boat that you row.
I've told you the story, do whatever you will.
It's past time for me to go!

Your Song

Make up a song.
Sing it loud and strong.
Fix it up any way that you want.

Sing it in the shower.
Or when you're sitting on the throne.
Sing it for your dog or cat.
Sing it all alone.

Sing it cause you're happy.
Sing it louder if you're not.
Don't be shy! Give it a try!
Just open your mouth
And let it all out.

Some people out there might say it's no good.
Keep singing because you know you should.

Don't get upset when there's no quartet,
To sing backup for whatever you've written.
Blow them a kiss and show them a smile.
Let them keep right on sitting.

You can sing well, your story tell,
Whether you're five or past fifty.
Get up and try, just make sure you don't die,
Before you share something nifty!

Make up a song.
Sing it loud and strong.
Do it for your own delight!
This is the part where you follow your heart.
The End is only the start . . . .